Langenscheidts
Verb-Tabellen
Englisch

herausgegeben von
der Langenscheidt Redaktion
bearbeitet von
Angela Einberger

Langenscheidt

Berlin · München · Wien · Zürich · New York

Herausgegeben von der Langenscheidt Redaktion
bearbeitet von Angela Einberger
Projektleitung und Redaktion: Christian Frieser

Auflage:	5.	4.	3.	2.	1.	Letzte Zahlen
Jahr:	03	02	01	2000		maßgeblich

© 2000 Langenscheidt KG, Berlin und München
Druck: Druckhaus Langenscheidt, Berlin-Schöneberg
Printed in Germany · ISBN 3-468-34121-0

Inhaltsverzeichnis

In der Konjugationsübersicht bedeutet das Zeichen:
+ = bejahend   **–** = verneinend   **+ ?** = fragend   **– ?** = fragend verneinend.
* seltene oder veraltete Form

Erklärung der wichtigsten englischen grammatischen Begriffe

active (voice) —————————— Aktiv (z. B. **I drive**)

American English (AE) — Amerikanisches Englisch

aspect —————————— Aspekt (einfache bzw. Verlaufsform)

auxiliary —————————— Hilfsverb (**to be, to have, to do**)

British English (BE) —————— Britisches Englisch

continuous form —————— Verlaufsform (siehe **progressive form**)

future —————————— Zukunft (**I will drive**)

gerund —————————— Gerundium (**driving**)

imperative —————————— Imperativ (Befehlsform)

indicative —————————— Indikativ

infinitive —————————— Infinitiv (Grundform, z. B. **to drive**)

irregular verbs —————— unregelmäßige Verben

modal auxiliary —————— modales Hilfsverb (**can, may, must,** usw.)

mood —————————— Modus (Indikativ, Konjunktiv oder Imperativ)

participle —————————— Partizip (**driving**)

passive (voice) —————— Passiv (z. B. **I am driven**)

past participle —————— Partizip Perfekt (3. Form des Verbs, z. B. **driven**)

past perfect —————————— Plusquamperfekt (z. B. **I had driven**)

past —————————— Vergangenheit

plural —————————— Plural (Mehrzahl)

present perfect —————— Perfekt (z. B. **I have driven**)

present —————————— Präsens (Gegenwart)

progressive form —————— Verlaufsform (s. a. **continuous** form, z. B. **I am/was driving**)

regular verbs —————— regelmäßige Verben

simple form —————————— Einfache Form (**I drive**)

singular —————————— Singular (Einzahl)

subjunctive —————————— Konjunktiv

tense —————————— Zeitform (**present, past,** etc.)

Hinweise für den Benutzer

Langenscheidts Verb-Tabellen Englisch bieten Ihnen einen systematischen Überblick über sämtliche Verbformen des Englischen. Wir beschränken uns dabei nicht auf die unregelmäßigen Verben, sondern geben in übersichtlichen Tabellen eine Gesamtdarstellung der englischen Konjugation für Voll- und Hilfsverben.

Das Buch besteht aus fünf Teilen. Im ersten Abschnitt erfahren Sie alles Wichtige zur Bildung der verschiedenen Verbformen sowie Grundsätzliches zur Verwendung der verschiedenen Zeitstufen (*tenses*). Außerdem machen wir Sie auf wichtige Besonderheiten z. B. in der Aussprache oder der Schreibweise aufmerksam.

Im zweiten Teil präsentieren wir Ihnen sämtliche mögliche Verbformen anhand des Beispielverbs *to drive*, wobei zunächst die einfachen (*simple forms*) und anschließend die Verlaufsformen (*progressive* bzw. *continuous forms*) aufgeführt werden. Jeder dieser beiden Teile untergliedert sich wiederum in einen ersten Teil mit Aktivformen und einen zweiten mit Passivformen.

Der dritte Abschnitt ordnet nach demselben Prinzip sämtliche Formen der vollständigen Hilfsverben (*auxiliaries*) *to be*, *to have* und *to do* an.

Die Formen der modalen Hilfsverben (*modal auxiliaries*) *can, may, must, shall, will, used to, ought to, need* und *dare* bzw. deren Ersatzverben bilden den vierten Teil dieses Überblicks.

Am Ende des Bandes finden Sie eine Liste sämtlicher unregelmäßiger Verben. Wollen Sie eine ganz bestimmte unregelmäßige Verbform nachschlagen, so können Sie dies im Anschluss daran in der alphabetischen Liste der einzelnen Stammformen tun.

Allgemeines
1. Übersicht über den Verbbestand

Man unterscheidet im Englischen nach

- der **Funktion** im Satz: **Vollverben** und **Hilfsverben**;
- der **Konjugation**: **starke** und **schwache Verben**, **regelmäßige** und **unregelmäßige Verben**;
- dem **Formenbestand**: **vollständige** und **unvollständige Hilfsverben**.

Vollverben		Beispiel		Bildung des past und des past participle	
schwach	regelmäßig	to look looked looked	[u] [u] [u]	auf **-ed**	
	unregelmäßig	to build built built	[i] [i] [i]	auf **-t**	ohne oder mit Veränderung des Stammvokals
		to hear heard heard	[iə] [əː] [əː]	auf **-d**	
		to tell told told	[e] [əu] [əu]		
stark	unregelmäßig	to give gave given	[i] [ei] [i]		durch Veränderung des Stammvokals

Vollständige Hilfsverben	Beispiel	Formenbestand
	to be	bilden alle Verbformen

Unvollständige Hilfsverben	Beispiel	Formenbestand
	can	bilden keine zusammengesetzten Zeiten, keinen Infinitiv, kein Partizip und Gerundium; ihnen folgt der Infinitiv ohne **to**

2. Zeiten und Verbformen

a) Die Zeitformen (tenses)

present	Präsens	Gegenwart
past	Präteritum	Vergangenheit
present perfect	formal: Perfekt	formal: Vorgegenwart
	Beachten Sie den unterschiedlichen Gebrauch von **pres. perf.** und deutschem Perfekt	
past perfect	Plusquamperfekt	Vorvergangenheit
future	1. Futur	Zukunft
future perfect	2. Futur	Vorzukunft
present conditional, future in the past	1. Konditional	1. Bedingungsform
perfect conditional, future perfect in the past	2. Konditional	2. Bedingungsform

Nach der **Bildungsweise** unterscheidet man:

Einfache Zeiten	**Zusammengesetzte Zeiten**
present	alle Zeiten des Aktivs außer **present** und **past**,
past	alle Zeiten des Passivs

Nach dem **Zeitbezug** unterscheidet man:

Zeiten der Gegenwart	**Zeiten der Vergangenheit**
present	**past**
present perfect	**past perfect**
future	**present conditional**
future perfect	**perfect conditional**

b) Die unbestimmten (infiniten) Verbformen

infinitive	Infinitiv
participle	Partizip
gerund	Gerundium

c) Die Zustandsformen

active	Aktiv
passive	Passiv

d) Die Aussageweise (mood)

indicative	Indikativ	Wirklichkeitsform
subjunctive	Konjunktiv	Möglichkeitsform
imperative	Imperativ	Befehlsform

e) Der Aspekt (aspect)

simple form	Einfache Form
continuous form/progressive form	Verlaufsform

3. Der Gebrauch der Zeiten

Das **present simple** bezeichnet einmalige oder immer wiederkehrende Handlungen oder Zustände, die an keine bestimmte Zeit gebunden sind:

He always has a cup of coffee after dinner.	Nach dem Essen trinkt er immer eine Tasse Kaffee.
He knows what to say.	Er weiß (immer), was er sagen soll.
The sun sets in the west.	Die Sonne geht (immer) im Westen unter.

(Soll ausgedrückt werden, dass eine Handlung zum Zeitpunkt des Sprechens stattfindet, so steht die **present continuous** Form, s. S. 9)

Das **present** steht oft **statt** des **future**, wenn der Satz eine Zeitangabe enthält, die auf die Zukunft hinweist:

He returns tomorrow.	Er kommt morgen zurück.
We start next week.	Wir fahren nächste Woche los.

Das **present** steht in zeitlichen und bedingenden Nebensätzen:

When ⎫ If ⎭ **he comes we'll tell him.**	Wenn ⎫ er kommt, werden wir es Falls ⎭ ihm sagen.

Das **past** drückt einen Vorgang aus, der abgeschlossen in der Vergangenheit liegt. Im Deutschen steht stattdessen häufig das Perfekt:

We met him yesterday.	Wir trafen ihn gestern/Wir haben ihn gestern getroffen.

Das **present perfect** drückt einen Vorgang aus, der in der Vergangenheit begann und in der Gegenwart andauert oder im Bewusstsein des Sprechenden in Beziehung zur Gegenwart steht:

How long have you been here?	Wie lange sind Sie (schon) hier?
I have read the book and I don't think it is too good.	Ich habe das Buch gelesen und finde es nicht besonders gut.

Das **past perfect** steht für Vorgänge, die vor anderen, im **past** ausgedrückten Vorgängen liegen:

I had read the book before I saw the film.	Bevor ich mir den Film ansah, hatte ich das Buch gelesen.
He had shut the windows before he left the house.	Er hatte die Fenster geschlossen, bevor er das Haus verließ.

Das **future** drückt zukünftige Vorgänge aus:
I hope we'll be there in time.   Hoffentlich sind wir rechtzeitig dort.

Statt des **future** steht in bestimmten Fällen das **present** (s. S. 8), die **present continuous form** (s. u.) oder **to be going to**.

4. Die continuous form

Die **continuous form** bzw. **progressive form** (Verlaufsform) bezeichnet einen Vorgang der zum Zeitpunkt des Sprechens stattfindet, während die entsprechende **simple form** nur die Tatsache, dass etwas vor sich geht (ging, gehen wird usw.), bezeichnet:

simple form	continuous form
He goes to school.	**He is going to school.**
Er geht (immer, regelmäßig) zur Schule = Er ist Schüler.	Er geht (gerade eben) zur Schule = Er ist auf dem Schulweg.

Die **continuous form** bezeichnet eine Handlung, die noch im Verlauf begriffen ist, während eine zweite Handlung einsetzt:
I was reading a book when I suddenly heard a noise.

Die **continuous form** bezeichnet die Gleichzeitigkeit zweier nebeneinander verlaufender Handlungen:
I was writing while my brother was reading a book.

Die **present continuous form** oder die Umschreibung mit **to be going to** drückt aus, dass etwas beabsichtigt ist oder in naher Zukunft geschehen wird.
He is buying a new car this week.   Er wird diese Woche ein neues Auto kaufen.

He is going to buy a new car.   Er ist im Begriff, ein neues Auto zu kaufen.

Die **continuous form** steht **nicht**
- bei ständig wiederholten Handlungen:
  I always get up at seven o'clock;
- bei Zuständen unbegrenzter Dauer:
  London is the capital of England;
- bei Verben, die keine Handlung, sondern einen Zustand, eine Sinneswahrnehmung oder eine innere Einstellung ausdrücken:
  We hope for better times.

Solche Verben sind u. a. **to know** wissen, **to hope** hoffen, **to feel** fühlen, **to fear** fürchten, **to seem** scheinen, den Anschein haben, **to understand** verstehen, **to like** gern mögen, **to love** lieben, **to belong to** gehören, **to possess** besitzen, **to consist of** bestehen aus.

9

5. Die Zeitenfolge

Für die Zeitenfolge ist die Unterscheidung von Zeiten der Gegenwart und Zeiten der Vergangenheit wichtig (s. S. 7).

Steht im übergeordneten Satz eine Zeit der Gegenwart, so steht im abhängigen Satz die Zeit, die in der direkten Rede stehen würde:

He says: "I arrived yesterday."   **He says (that) he arrived yesterday.**

Steht im übergeordneten Satz eine Zeit der Vergangenheit, so werden im abhängigen Satz die Zeiten wie folgt verschoben:

present   →   **past**
He said: "I see him often."   He said (that) he saw him often.

past   →   **past perfect**
He said: "I saw him last week."   He said (that) he had seen him the
                                         week before.

present perfect   →   **past perfect**
He said: "I have been in London   He said (that) he had been in
   for three days"   London for three days.

future   →   **conditional**
He said: "I will return soon"   He said (that) he would return soon.

6. Vollform : Kurzform

Die in den Konjugationsübersichten aufgeführten Kurzformen werden im Allgemeinen in der gesprochenen Sprache verwendet. In der geschriebenen Sprache bevorzugt man überwiegend die Vollformen. Beispiele:

Geschrieben	Gesprochen
He cannot	**He can't**
He would not	**He wouldn't** oder **He'd not**

Je nach Stilebene finden die Kurzformen auch in der geschriebenen Sprache unterschiedliche Verbreitung.

Die zweite Kurzform, bei der „not" nicht abgekürzt wird, ist weniger gebräuchlich. Sie findet meist dann Verwendung, wenn „not" besonders betont werden soll.

Bei der schriftlichen Wiedergabe der direkten Rede werden ebenfalls die Kurzformen verwendet.

7. Frage und Verneinung

Frage und Verneinung mit „not" im **present** und **past** der Vollverben werden mit **to do** gebildet:

Frage: **Do you drive?**   Verneinung: **I do not drive.**
       Did he drive?   **He did not drive.**

Keine Umschreibung mit **to do** erfolgt, wenn
- das Prädikat ein Hilfsverb enthält (also auch bei allen zusammengesetzten Zeiten): **Have you driven? – He has not driven. – Can he drive?;**
- in nicht mit „not" verneinten Fragesätzen das Fragewort Subjekt oder Attribut des Subjekts ist: **Who got the book? – Whose book lies on the table? – Which book lies on the table?**

8. Besonderheiten in Aussprache und Schreibung

a) Endung –s in der 3. Person Singular **present simple**

Die Endung **-s** wird gesprochen:
- nach stimmlosen Konsonanten stimmlos [-s];
- nach stimmhaften Konsonanten und Vokalen stimmhaft [-z]:
    to get [get]   **to run** [rʌn]   **to see** [siː]
    he gets [gets]   **he runs** [rʌnz]   **he sees** [siːz]
- Bei Verben, die auf einem Zischlaut ([s], [z], [(t)ʃ], [(d)ʒ]) enden, wird die 3. Person Singular **present simple** als [-iz] hörbar:
    to judge [dʒʌdʒ]   **to rise** [raiz]
    he judges ['dʒʌdʒiz]   **he rises** ['raiziz]

    Ausnahme:
    to do   [duː]
    he does [dʌz]

Die Endung in der 3. Person Singular **simple present** wird geschrieben:
- **-s** bei den meisten Verben
- **-es** bei Verben auf **-s, -z, -ch, -sh, -x, -o**
    to hiss   **to catch**   **to wish**   **to go**
    he hisses   **he catches**   **he wishes**   **he goes**
- Verben, die auf Konsonant + **-y** enden, verwandeln das **-y** in **-i** und bilden die 3. Person Singular **present simple** auf **-es** [-z]:
    to carry   ['kæri]
    he carries ['kæriz]

    Aber **-y** nach Vokal bleibt erhalten:
    to play [plei]
    he plays [pleiz]

b) Endung **-ed** im **past** und **past participle**

Die Endung **-ed** wird gesprochen:
- nach stimmlosen Konsonanten stimmlos [-t];
- nach stimmhaften Konsonanten und Vokalen stimmhaft [-d];
- nach **-d** und **-t** silbisch [-id]:

to look	[luk]	**to gain**	[gein]	**to show**	[ʃəu]
he looked	[lukt]	**he gained**	[geind]	**he showed**	[ʃəud]

to add	[æd]	**to fit**	[fit]
he added	['ædid]	**it fitted**	['fitid]

Verben, die auf Konsonant + **-y** enden, verwandeln das **-y** vor **-ed** zu **i-**:
to cry [krai]   **he cried** [kraid]

Aber **-y** nach Vokal bleibt erhalten:
to play [plei]   **he played** [pleid]

Verben, die auf stummem **-e** enden, bilden **past** und **past participle** durch Anhängen von **-d** statt **-ed**:
to move [muːv]   **he moved** [muːvd]

Endkonsonanten werden vor **-ed** verdoppelt, wenn sie in betonter Silbe stehen und auf einen einfach geschriebenen Vokal folgen:

to stop	[stɔp]	Aber: **to look**	[luk]	(Vokal durch 2 Buch-	
he stopped	[stɔpt]	**he looked**	[lukt]	staben wiedergegeben!)	

to prefer	[priˈfəː]	Aber: **to enter**	['entə]	(Vokal in unbetonter	
he preferred	[priˈfəːd]	**he entered**	['entəd]	Silbe!)	

Ein **-l** am Wortende, das auf einen kurzen Vokal folgt, wird im britischen Englisch auch in unbetonter Silbe vor **-ed** verdoppelt:
to travel   ['trævl]
he travelled   ['trævld] AE: **he traveled**

c) Endung **-ing** im **present participle** und **gerund**

- In Verben, die auf **-ie** enden, wird **-ie** vor **-ing** zu **-y**:
  to lie [lai]   **lying** ['laiiŋ]
- Verben, die auf **stummem -e** enden, verlieren dieses **-e** vor **-ing**:
  to move [muːv]   **moving** ['muːviŋ]

Endkonsonanten werden vor **-ing** verdoppelt, wenn sie in betonter Silbe stehen und auf einen einfach geschriebenen Vokal folgen:

to stop	[stɔp]	Aber: **to look**	[luk]	(Vokal durch 2 Buch-	
stopping	['stɔpiŋ]	**looking**	['lukiŋ]	staben wiedergegeben!)	
to prefer	[priˈfəː]	Aber: **to enter**	['entə]	(Vokal in unbetonter	
preferring	[priˈfəːriŋ]	**entering**	['entəriŋ]	Silbe!)	

Ein **-l** am Wortende, das auf einen kurzen Vokal folgt, wird im britischen Englisch auch in unbetonter Silbe vor **-ing** verdoppelt:
to travel ['trævl]   **travelling** ['trævliŋ] AE: **traveling**

Vollverben • 1. simple forms

active

	present	past	perfect
infinitive	**to drive** fahren		**to have driven** gefahren sein
participle	**driving** wörtl. „fahrend"; wird am Satzanfang mit kausalem/temporalem Nebensatz übersetzt (da/während er/sie … fuhr)	**driven** gefahren	**having driven** wird im Deutschen meist mit kausalem/temporalem Nebensatz wiedergegeben (da/nachdem er/sie gefahren war)
gerund	**driving** (das) Fahren		**having driven** häufiger wird auf die Form **gerund present** zurückgegriffen: **The man was accused of driving** (statt: **having driven**) **too fast.**

imperative

bejahend	**drive** fahr(e)/fahrt/fahren Sie!
betont	**do drive** fahr(e)/fahrt/fahren Sie doch!
verneinend	**do not drive/don't drive** fahr(e)/fahrt/fahren Sie nicht!

passive

	present	past	perfect
infinitive	**to be driven** gefahren werden		**to have been driven** gefahren worden sein
participle	**being driven** wörtl. „gefahren werdend"; wird am Satzanfang mit kausalem/temporalem Nebensatz wiedergegeben (da/während er/sie gefahren wurde)	**driven** gefahren	**having been driven** wird im Deutschen meist mit kausalem/temporalem Nebensatz wiedergegeben (da/nachdem er/sie gefahren worden war)
gerund	**being driven** wörtl. „(das) Gefahrenwerden"; wird im Deutschen aber meist mit Infinitiv übersetzt (gefahren zu werden)		**having been driven** häufiger wird auf die Form **gerund present** zurückgegriffen

Vollverben

a) active

present simple active

ich fahre +

I	drive
you	drive
he	drives
she	drives
it	drives
we	drive
you	drive
they	drive

ich fahre nicht −

I	don't	drive		I	do	not drive
you	don't	drive		you	do	not drive
he	doesn't	drive		he	does	not drive
she	doesn't	drive		she	does	not drive
it	doesn't	drive		it	does	not drive
we	don't	drive		we	do	not drive
you	don't	drive		you	do	not drive
they	don't	drive		they	do	not drive

fahre ich? + ?

do	I	drive?
	you	drive?
does	he	drive?
	she	drive?
	it	drive?
do	we	drive?
	you	drive?
	they	drive?

fahre ich nicht? − ?

don't	I	drive?		do	I	not drive?
	you	drive?			you	not drive?
doesn't	he	drive?		does	he	not drive?
	she	drive?			she	not drive?
	it	drive?			it	not drive?
don't	we	drive?		do	we	not drive?
	you	drive?			you	not drive?
	they	drive?			they	not drive?

past simple active

ich fuhr

I	drove
you	drove
he	drove
she	drove
it	drove
we	drove
you	drove
they	drove

ich fuhr nicht

I	didn't drive	I	did not drive
you	didn't drive	you	did not drive
he	didn't drive	he	did not drive
she	didn't drive	she	did not drive
it	didn't drive	it	did not drive
we	didn't drive	we	did not drive
you	didn't drive	you	did not drive
they	didn't drive	they	did not drive

fuhr ich?

did	I	drive?
	you	drive?
	he	drive?
	she	drive?
	it	drive?
	we	drive?
	you	drive?
	they	drive?

fuhr ich nicht?

didn't	I	drive?	did	I	not drive?
	you	drive?		you	not drive?
	he	drive?		he	not drive?
	she	drive?		she	not drive?
	it	drive?		it	not drive?
	we	drive?		we	not drive?
	you	drive?		you	not drive?
	they	drive?		they	not drive?

Vollverben

present perfect simple active

present von **to have** + **past participle**

ich bin gefahren/ich fahre (seit)   +

I've	driven		I	have	driven
you've	driven		you	have	driven
he's	driven		he	has	driven
she's	driven		she	has	driven
it's	driven		it	has	driven
we've	driven		we	have	driven
you've	driven		you	have	driven
they've	driven		they	have	driven

ich bin (noch) nicht gefahren   —

I	haven't	driven		I	have	not driven
you	haven't	driven		you	have	not driven
he	hasn't	driven		he	has	not driven
she	hasn't	driven		she	has	not driven
it	hasn't	driven		it	has	not driven
we	haven't	driven		we	have	not driven
you	haven't	driven		you	have	not driven
they	haven't	driven		they	have	not driven

Daneben sind auch die Kurzformen
I've not driven, etc. gebräuchlich.

bin ich (schon) gefahren?   + ?

have	I	driven?
	you	driven?
has	he	driven?
	she	driven?
	it	driven?
have	we	driven?
	you	driven?
	they	driven?

bin ich (noch) nicht gefahren?   − ?

haven't	I	driven?	have	I	not driven?
	you	driven?		you	not driven?
hasn't	he	driven?	has	he	not driven?
	she	driven?		she	not driven?
	it	driven?		it	not driven?
haven't	we	driven?	have	we	not driven?
	you	driven?		you	not driven?
	they	driven?		they	not driven?

past perfect simple active

past von **to have** + **past participle**

ich war gefahren   +

I'd	driven	I	had driven
you'd	driven	you	had driven
he'd	driven	he	had driven
she'd	driven	she	had driven
it'd	driven	it	had driven
we'd	driven	we	had driven
you'd	driven	you	had driven
they'd	driven	they	had driven

ich war nicht gefahren   –

I	hadn't driven	I	had not driven
you	hadn't driven	you	had not driven
he	hadn't driven	he	had not driven
she	hadn't driven	she	had not driven
it	hadn't driven	it	had not driven
we	hadn't driven	we	had not driven
you	hadn't driven	you	had not driven
they	hadn't driven	they	had not driven

Daneben sind auch die Kurzformen
I'd not driven, etc. gebräuchlich.

war ich gefahren?   + ?

had	I	driven?
	you	driven?
	he	driven?
	she	driven?
	it	driven?
	we	driven?
	you	driven?
	they	driven?

war ich nicht gefahren?   – ?

hadn't	I	driven?	had	I	not driven?
	you	driven?		you	not driven?
	he	driven?		he	not driven?
	she	driven?		she	not driven?
	it	driven?		it	not driven?
	we	driven?		we	not driven?
	you	driven?		you	not driven?
	they	driven?		they	not driven?

Vollverben

future simple active

will/*shall + infinitive

Die mit * gekennzeichnete Form **shall** ist heute kaum mehr gebräuchlich.

ich werde fahren   +

I'll	drive	I	will/*shall drive
you'll	drive	you	will drive
he'll	drive	he	will drive
she'll	drive	she	will drive
it'll	drive	it	will drive
we'll	drive	we	will/*shall drive
you'll	drive	you	will drive
they'll	drive	they	will drive

ich werde nicht fahren   –

I	won't/*shan't drive	I	will/*shall not drive
you	won't drive	you	will not drive
he	won't drive	he	will not drive
she	won't drive	she	will not drive
it	won't drive	it	will not drive
we	won't/*shan't drive	we	will/*shall not drive
you	won't drive	you	will not drive
they	won't drive	they	will not drive

Daneben sind auch die Kurzformen **I'll not drive**, etc. gebräuchlich.

werde ich fahren?   + ?

will/*shall	I	drive?
will	you	drive?
	he	drive?
	she	drive?
	it	drive?
will/*shall	we	drive?
will	you	drive?
	they	drive?

werde ich nicht fahren?   – ?

won't/ *shan't	I	drive?	will/ *shall	I	not drive?
won't	you	drive?	will	you	not drive?
usw.			usw.		

Anstatt mit **will + infinitive** kann das **future simple active** auch mit **to be going to + infinitive** gebildet werden. Dabei wird nur das Hilfsverb **to be** (siehe dort) entsprechend konjugiert.

future perfect simple active

will/*shall + perfect infinitive

ich werde gefahren sein   +

I'll	have driven		I	will/*shall have driven
you'll	have driven		you	will have driven
he'll	have driven		he	will have driven
she'll	have driven		she	will have driven
it'll	have driven		it	will have driven
we'll	have driven		we	will/*shall have driven
you'll	have driven		you	will have driven
they'll	have driven		they	will have driven

ich werde nicht gefahren sein   –

I	won't/*shan't have driven		I	will/*shall not have driven
you	won't have driven		you	will not have driven
he	won't have driven		he	will not have driven
she	won't have driven		she	will not have driven
it	won't have driven		it	will not have driven
we	won't/*shan't have driven		we	will/*shall not have driven
you	won't have driven		you	will not have driven
they	won't have driven		they	will not have driven

Daneben sind auch die Kurzformen
I'll not have driven, etc. gebräuchlich.

werde ich gefahren sein?   + ?

will/*shall	I	have driven?
will	you	have driven?
	he	have driven?
	she	have driven?
	it	have driven?
will/*shall	we	have driven?
will	you	have driven?
	they	have driven?

werde ich nicht gefahren sein?   – ?

won't/ *shan't	I	have driven?	will/ *shall	I	not have driven?
won't	you	have driven?	will	you	not have driven?
	he	have driven?		he	not have driven?
	she	have driven?		she	not have driven?
	it	have driven?		it	not have driven?
won't/ *shan't	we	have driven?	will/ *shall	we	not have driven?
won't	you	have driven?	will	you	not have driven?
	they	have driven?		they	not have driven?

Vollverben

present conditional/future in the past simple active

would/*should + infinitive   ***should** in der Funktion des Konditionals
ist heute nicht mehr gebräuchlich

ich würde fahren

I'd	drive	I	would/*should drive
you'd	drive	you	would drive
he'd	drive	he	would drive
she'd	drive	she	would drive
it'd	drive	it	would drive
we'd	drive	we	would/*should drive
you'd	drive	you	would drive
they'd	drive	they	would drive

ich würde nicht fahren

I	wouldn't/*shouldn't drive	I	would/*should not drive
you	wouldn't drive	you	would not drive
he	wouldn't drive	he	would not drive
she	wouldn't drive	she	would not drive
it	wouldn't drive	it	would not drive
we	wouldn't/*shouldn't drive	we	would/*should not drive
you	wouldn't drive	you	would not drive
they	wouldn't drive	they	would not drive

Daneben sind auch die Kurzformen
I'd not drive, etc. gebräuchlich.

würde ich fahren?

would/*should	I	drive?
would	you	drive?
	he	drive?
	she	drive?
	it	drive?
would/*should	we	drive?
would	you	drive?
	they	drive?

würde ich nicht fahren?

wouldn't/ *shouldn't	I	drive?	would/ *should	I	not drive?
wouldn't	you	drive?	would	you	not drive?
usw.			usw.		

Anstatt mit „would" + **infinitive** kann das **future in the past simple
active** (nicht das **present conditional**!) auch mit „**was/were going to**"
+ **infinitive** gebildet werden. Dabei wird nur das Hilfsverb „**was/were**"
(siehe „**to be**") entsprechend konjugiert.

perfect conditional – future perfect in the past simple active

would/*should + perfect infinitive

ich wäre gefahren   +

I'd	have driven	I	would/*should have driven
you'd	have driven	you	would have driven
he'd	have driven	he	would have driven
she'd	have driven	she	would have driven
it'd	have driven	it	would have driven
we'd	have driven	we	would/*should have driven
you'd	have driven	you	would have driven
they'd	have driven	they	would have driven

ich wäre nicht gefahren   −

I	wouldn't/*shouldn't have driven	I	would/*should not have driven
you	wouldn't have driven	you	would not have driven
he	wouldn't have driven	he	would not have driven
she	wouldn't have driven	she	would not have driven
it	wouldn't have driven	it	would not have driven
we	wouldn't/*shouldn't have driven	we	would/*should not have driven
you	wouldn't have driven	you	would not have driven
they	wouldn't have driven	they	would not have driven

Daneben sind auch die Kurzformen
I'd not have driven, etc. gebräuchlich.

wäre ich gefahren?   + ?

would/*should	I	have driven?
would	you	have driven?
	he	have driven?
	she	have driven?
	it	have driven?
would/*should	we	have driven?
would	you	have driven?
	they	have driven?

wäre ich nicht gefahren?   − ?

wouldn't/*shouldn't	I	have driven?	would/*should	I	not have driven?
wouldn't	you	have driven?	would	you	not have driven?
usw.			usw.		

Vollverben

21

b) passive

present simple passive

present von **to be** + **past participle**

ich werde gefahren

I'm	driven		I	am	driven
you're	driven		you	are	driven
he's	driven		he	is	driven
she's	driven		she		driven
it's	driven		it		driven
we're	driven		we	are	driven
you're	driven		you		driven
they're	driven		they		driven

ich werde nicht gefahren

I'm	not	driven		I	am	not driven
you	aren't	driven		you	are	not driven
he	isn't	driven		he	is	not driven
she		driven		she		not driven
it		driven		it		not driven
we	aren't	driven		we	are	not driven
you		driven		you		not driven
they		driven		they		not driven

Daneben sind auch die Kurzformen
you're not driven, etc. gebräuchlich.

werde ich gefahren?

am	I	driven?
are	you	driven?
is	he	driven?
	she	driven?
	it	driven?
are	we	driven?
	you	driven?
	they	driven?

werde ich nicht gefahren?

aren't	I	driven?	am	I	not driven?
	you	driven?	are	you	not driven?
isn't	he	driven?	is	he	not driven?
	she	driven?		she	not driven?
	it	driven?		it	not driven?
aren't	we	driven?	are	we	not driven?
	you	driven?		you	not driven?
	they	driven?		they	not driven?

past simple passive

ich wurde gefahren

I	was	driven
you	were	driven
he	was	driven
she	was	driven
it	was	driven
we	were	driven
you	were	driven
they	were	driven

ich wurde nicht gefahren

I	wasn't	driven		I	was	not driven
you	weren't	driven		you	were	not driven
he	wasn't	driven		he	was	not driven
she	wasn't	driven		she	was	not driven
it	wasn't	driven		it	was	not driven
we	weren't	driven		we	were	not driven
you	weren't	driven		you	were	not driven
they	weren't	driven		they	were	not driven

wurde ich gefahren?

was	I	driven?
were	you	driven?
was	he	driven?
	she	driven?
	it	driven?
were	we	driven?
	you	driven?
	they	driven?

wurde ich nicht gefahren?

wasn't	I	driven?		was	I	not driven?
weren't	you	driven?		were	you	not driven?
wasn't	he	driven?		was	he	not driven?
	she	driven?			she	not driven?
	it	driven?			it	not driven?
weren't	we	driven?		were	we	not driven?
	you	driven?			you	not driven?
	they	driven?			they	not driven?

Vollverben

present perfect simple passive

present perfect von **to be** + past participle

ich bin gefahren worden/werde (seit ...) gefahren   **+**

I've	been driven		I	have	been driven
you've	been driven		you	have	been driven
he's	been driven		he	has	been driven
she's	been driven		she	has	been driven
it's	been driven		it	has	been driven
we've	been driven		we	have	been driven
you've	been driven		you	have	been driven
they've	been driven		they	have	been driven

ich bin (noch) nicht gefahren worden   **–**

I	haven't	been driven	I	have	not been driven
you	haven't	been driven	you	have	not been driven
he	hasn't	been driven	he	has	not been driven
she	hasn't	been driven	she	has	not been driven
it	hasn't	been driven	it	has	not been driven
we	haven't	been driven	we	have	not been driven
you	haven't	been driven	you	have	not been driven
they	haven't	been driven	they	have	not been driven

Daneben sind auch die Kurzformen
I've not been driven, etc. gebräuchlich.

bin ich (schon) gefahren worden?   **+ ?**

have	I	been driven?
	you	been driven?
has	he	been driven?
	she	been driven?
	it	been driven?
have	we	been driven?
	you	been driven?
	they	been driven?

bin ich (noch) nicht gefahren worden?   **– ?**

haven't	I	been driven?	have	I	not been driven?
	you	been driven?		you	not been driven?
hasn't	he	been driven?	has	he	not been driven?
	she	been driven?		she	not been driven?
	it	been driven?		it	not been driven?
haven't	we	been driven?	have	we	not been driven?
	you	been driven?		you	not been driven?
	they	been driven?		they	not been driven?

past perfect simple passive

past perfect von **to be** + **past participle**

ich war gefahren worden ➕

I'd	been driven	I	had been driven
you'd	been driven	you	had been driven
he'd	been driven	he	had been driven
she'd	been driven	she	had been driven
it'd	been driven	it	had been driven
we'd	been driven	we	had been driven
you'd	been driven	you	had been driven
they'd	been driven	they	had been driven

ich war nicht gefahren worden ➖

I	hadn't been driven	I	had not been driven
you	hadn't been driven	you	had not been driven
he	hadn't been driven	he	had not been driven
she	hadn't been driven	she	had not been driven
it	hadn't been driven	it	had not been driven
we	hadn't been driven	we	had not been driven
you	hadn't been driven	you	had not been driven
they	hadn't been driven	they	had not been driven

Daneben sind auch die Kurzformen
I'd not been driven, etc. gebräuchlich.

war ich gefahren worden? ➕ ?

had	I	been driven?
	you	been driven?
	he	been driven?
	she	been driven?
	it	been driven?
	we	been driven?
	you	been driven?
	they	been driven?

war ich nicht gefahren worden? ➖ ?

hadn't	I	been driven?	had	I	not been driven?
	you	been driven?		you	not been driven?
	he	been driven?		he	not been driven?
	she	been driven?		she	not been driven?
	it	been driven?		it	not been driven?
	we	been driven?		we	not been driven?
	you	been driven?		you	not been driven?
	they	been driven?		they	not been driven?

Vollverben

future simple passive

will/*shall + infinitive passive

ich werde gefahren werden

+

I'll	be driven		I	will/*shall be driven
you'll	be driven		you	will be driven
he'll	be driven		he	will be driven
she'll	be driven		she	will be driven
it'll	be driven		it	will be driven
we'll	be driven		we	will/*shall be driven
you'll	be driven		you	will be driven
they'll	be driven		they	will be driven

ich werde nicht gefahren werden

−

I	won't/*shan't be driven		I	will/*shall not be driven
you	won't be driven		you	will not be driven
he	won't be driven		he	will not be driven
she	won't be driven		she	will not be driven
it	won't be driven		it	will not be driven
we	won't/*shan't be driven		we	will/*shall not be driven
you	won't be driven		you	will not be driven
they	won't be driven		they	will not be driven

Daneben sind auch die Kurzformen
I'll not be driven, etc. gebräuchlich.

werde ich gefahren werden?

+ ?

will/*shall	I	be driven?
will	you	be driven?
	he	be driven?
	she	be driven?
	it	be driven?
will/*shall	we	be driven?
will	you	be driven?
	they	be driven?

werde ich nicht gefahren werden?

− ?

won't/			will/		
*shan't	I	be driven	*shall	I	not be driven?
won't	you	be driven	will	you	not be driven?
usw.			usw.		

Anstatt mit „will" + **infinitive passive** kann das **future simple passive**
auch mit „to be going to" + **infinitive passive** gebildet werden. Dabei wird
nur das Hilfsverb **„to be"** (siehe dort) entsprechend konjugiert.

Vollverben (Seitenmarkierung)

future perfect simple passive

will/*shall + perfect infinitive passive

ich werde gefahren worden sein   +

I'll	have been driven	I	will/*shall have been driven
you'll	have been driven	you	will have been driven
he'll	have been driven	he	will have been driven
she'll	have been driven	she	will have been driven
it'll	have been driven	it	will have been driven
we'll	have been driven	we	will/*shall have been driven
you'll	have been driven	you	will have been driven
they'll	have been driven	they	will have been driven

ich werde nicht gefahren worden sein   –

I	won't/*shan't have been driven	I	will/*shall not have been driven
you	won't have been driven	you	will not have been driven
he	won't have been driven	he	will not have been driven
she	won't have been driven	she	will not have been driven
it	won't have been driven	it	will not have been driven
we	won't/*shan't have been driven	we	will/*shall not have been driven
you	won't have been driven	you	will not have been driven
they	won't have been driven	they	will not have been driven

Daneben sind auch die Kurzformen
I'll not have been driven, etc. gebräuchlich.

werde ich gefahren worden sein?   + ?

will/*shall	I	have been driven?
will	you	have been driven?
	he	have been driven?
	she	have been driven?
	it	have been driven?
will/*shall	we	have been driven?
will	you	have been driven?
	they	have been driven?

werde ich nicht gefahren worden sein?   – ?

won't/ *shan't	I	have been driven?	will/ *shall	I	not have been driven?
won't	you	have been driven?	will	you	not have been driven?
usw.			usw.		

Vollverben

27

present conditional/future in the past simple passive

would/*should + infinitive passive

ich würde gefahren werden

I'd	be driven	I	would/*should be driven
you'd	be driven	you	would be driven
he'd	be driven	he	would be driven
she'd	be driven	she	would be driven
it'd	be driven	it	would be driven
we'd	be driven	we	would/*should be driven
you'd	be driven	you	would be driven
they'd	be driven	they	would be driven

ich würde nicht gefahren werden

I	wouldn't/*shouldn't be driven	I	would/*should not be driven
you	wouldn't be driven	you	would not be driven
he	wouldn't be driven	he	would not be driven
she	wouldn't be driven	she	would not be driven
it	wouldn't be driven	it	would not be driven
we	wouldn't/*shouldn't be driven	we	would/*should not be driven
you	wouldn't be driven	you	would not be driven
they	wouldn't be driven	they	would not be driven

Daneben sind auch die Kurzformen
I'd not be driven, etc. gebräuchlich.

würde ich gefahren werden?

would/*should	I	be driven?
would	you	be driven?
	he	be driven?
	she	be driven?
	it	be driven?
would/*should	we	be driven?
would	you	be driven?
	they	be driven?

würde ich nicht gefahren werden?

wouldn't/*shouldn't	I	be driven?	would/*should	I	not be driven?
wouldn't	you	be driven?	would	you	not be driven?
usw.			usw.		

Anstatt mit „would" + **infinitive passive** kann das **future in the past
simple passive** (nicht das **present conditional**!) auch mit „was/were
going to" + **infinitive passive** gebildet werden. Dabei wird nur das Hilfsverb „was/were" (siehe „to be") entsprechend konjugiert.

perfect conditional/future perfect in the past simple passive

would/*should + perfect infinitive passive

ich wäre gefahren worden

I'd	have been driven	I	would/*should have been driven
you'd	have been driven	you	would have been driven
he'd	have been driven	he	would have been driven
she'd	have been driven	she	would have been driven
it'd	have been driven	it	would have been driven
we'd	have been driven	we	would/*should have been driven
you'd	have been driven	you	would have been driven
they'd	have been driven	they	would have been driven

ich wäre nicht gefahren worden

I	wouldn't/*shouldn't have been driven	I	would/*should not have been driven
you	wouldn't have been driven	you	would not have been driven
he	wouldn't have been driven	he	would not have been driven
she	wouldn't have been driven	she	would not have been driven
it	wouldn't have been driven	it	would not have been driven
we	wouldn't/*shouldn't have been driven	we	would/*should not have been driven
you	wouldn't have been driven	you	would not have been driven
they	wouldn't have been driven	they	would not have been driven

Daneben sind auch die Kurzformen
I'd not have been driven, etc. gebräuchlich.

wäre ich gefahren worden?

would/*should	I	have been driven?
would	you	have been driven?
	he	have been driven?
	she	have been driven?
	it	have been driven?
would/*should	we	have been driven?
would	you	have been driven?
	they	have been driven?

wäre ich nicht gefahren worden?

wouldn't/ *shouldn't	I	have been driven?	would/ *should	I	not have been driven?
wouldn't	you	have been driven?	would	you	not have been driven?
usw.			usw.		

2. continuous forms

active

	present	perfect
infinitive	**to be driving** fahren	**to have been driving** gefahren sein

Infinite Formen im **continuous passive** gibt es nicht.

a) active

present continuous active

present von **to be + present participle**

ich fahre

I'm	driving		I	am	driving
you're	driving		you	are	driving
he's	driving		he	is	driving
she's	driving		she	is	driving
it's	driving		it	is	driving
we're	driving		we	are	driving
you're	driving		you	are	driving
they're	driving		they	are	driving

ich fahre nicht

I'm	not	driving		I	am	not driving
you	aren't	driving		you	are	not driving
he	isn't	driving		he	is	not driving
usw.				usw.		

Daneben sind auch die Kurzformen
you're not driving, etc. gebräuchlich.

fahre ich?

am	I	driving?
are	you	driving?
usw.		

fahre ich nicht?

aren't	I	driving?		am	I	not driving?
	you	driving?		are	you	not driving?
isn't	he	driving?		is	he	not driving?
usw.				usw.		

past continuous active

past von **to be** + **present participle**

ich fuhr

+

I	was	driving
you	were	driving
he	was	driving
she	was	driving
it	was	driving
we	were	driving
you	were	driving
they	were	driving

ich fuhr nicht

−

I	wasn't	driving	I	was	not driving
you	weren't	driving	you	were	not driving
he	wasn't	driving	he	was	not driving
she	wasn't	driving	she	was	not driving
it	wasn't	driving	it	was	not driving
we	weren't	driving	we	were	not driving
you	weren't	driving	you	were	not driving
they	weren't	driving	they	were	not driving

fuhr ich?

+ ?

was	I	driving?
were	you	driving?
was	he	driving?
	she	driving?
	it	driving?
were	we	driving?
	you	driving?
	they	driving?

fuhr ich nicht?

− ?

wasn't	I	driving?	was	I	not driving?
weren't	you	driving?	were	you	not driving?
wasn't	he	driving?	was	he	not driving?
	she	driving?		she	not driving?
	it	driving?		it	not driving?
weren't	we	driving?	were	we	not driving?
	you	driving?		you	not driving?
	they	driving?		they	not driving?

Vollverben

present perfect continuous active

present perfect von **to be** + **present participle**

ich bin gefahren/ich fahre (schon seit)   **+**

I've	been driving	I	have	been driving
you've	been driving	you	have	been driving
he's	been driving	he	has	been driving
she's	been driving	she	has	been driving
it's	been driving	it	has	been driving
we've	been driving	we	have	been driving
you've	been driving	you	have	been driving
they've	been driving	they	have	been driving

ich bin (noch) nicht gefahren   **–**

I	haven't	been driving	I	have	not been driving
you	haven't	been driving	you	have	not been driving
he	hasn't	been driving	he	has	not been driving
she	hasn't	been driving	she	has	not been driving
it	hasn't	been driving	it	has	not been driving
we	haven't	been driving	we	have	not been driving
you	haven't	been driving	you	have	not been driving
they	haven't	been driving	they	have	not been driving

Daneben sind auch die Kurzformen
I've not been driving, etc. gebräuchlich.

bin ich (schon) gefahren?   **+ ?**

have	I	been driving?
	you	been driving?
has	he	been driving?
	she	been driving?
	it	been driving?
have	we	been driving?
	you	been driving?
	they	been driving?

bin ich (noch) nicht gefahren?   **– ?**

haven't	I	been driving?	have	I	not been driving?
	you	been driving?		you	not been driving?
hasn't	he	been driving?	has	he	not been driving?
	she	been driving?		she	not been driving?
	it	been driving?		it	not been driving?
haven't	we	been driving?	have	we	not been driving?
	you	been driving?		you	not been driving?
	they	been driving?		they	not been driving?

past perfect continuous active

past perfect von **to be** + **present participle**

ich war gefahren +

I'd	been driving	I	had been driving
you'd	been driving	you	had been driving
he'd	been driving	he	had been driving
she'd	been driving	she	had been driving
it'd	been driving	it	had been driving
we'd	been driving	we	had been driving
you'd	been driving	you	had been driving
they'd	been driving	they	had been driving

ich war nicht gefahren −

I	hadn't been driving	I	had not been driving
you	hadn't been driving	you	had not been driving
he	hadn't been driving	he	had not been driving
she	hadn't been driving	she	had not been driving
it	hadn't been driving	it	had not been driving
we	hadn't been driving	we	had not been driving
you	hadn't been driving	you	had not been driving
they	hadn't been driving	they	had not been driving

Daneben sind auch die Kurzformen
I'd not been driving, etc. gebräuchlich.

war ich gefahren? + ?

had	I	been driving?
	you	been driving?
	he	been driving?
	she	been driving?
	it	been driving?
	we	been driving?
	you	been driving?
	they	been driving?

war ich nicht gefahren? − ?

hadn't	I	been driving?	had	I	not been driving?
	you	been driving?		you	not been driving?
	he	been driving?		he	not been driving?
	she	been driving?		she	not been driving?
	it	been driving?		it	not been driving?
	we	been driving?		we	not been driving?
	you	been driving?		you	not been driving?
	they	been driving?		they	not been driving?

Vollverben

future continuous active

future von **to be + present participle**

ich werde fahren

I'll	be driving	I	will/*shall be driving
you'll	be driving	you	will be driving
he'll	be driving	he	will be driving
she'll	be driving	she	will be driving
it'll	be driving	it	will be driving
we'll	be driving	we	will/*shall be driving
you'll	be driving	you	will be driving
they'll	be driving	they	will be driving

ich werde nicht fahren

I	won't/*shan't be driving	I	will/*shall not be driving
you	won't be driving	you	will not be driving
he	won't be driving	he	will not be driving
she	won't be driving	she	will not be driving
it	won't be driving	it	will not be driving
we	won't/*shan't be driving	we	will/*shall not be driving
you	won't be driving	you	will not be driving
they	won't be driving	they	will not be driving

Daneben sind auch die Kurzformen
I'll not be driving, etc. gebräuchlich.

werde ich fahren?

will/*shall	I	be driving?
will	you	be driving?
	he	be driving?
	she	be driving?
	it	be driving?
will/*shall	we	be driving?
will	you	be driving?
	they	be driving?

werde ich nicht fahren?

won't/*shan't	I	be driving?	will/*shall	I	not be driving?
won't	you	be driving?	will	you	not be driving?
	he	be driving?		he	not be driving?
	she	be driving?		she	not be driving?
	it	be driving?		it	not be driving?
won't/*shan't	we	be driving?	will/*shall	we	not be driving?
won't	you	be driving?	will	you	not be driving?
	they	be driving?		they	not be driving?

future perfect continuous active

future perfect von **to be** + **present participle**

ich werde gefahren sein   +

I'll	have been driving	I	will/*shall have been driving
you'll	have been driving	you	will have been driving
he'll	have been driving	he	will have been driving
she'll	have been driving	she	will have been driving
it'll	have been driving	it	will have been driving
we'll	have been driving	we	will/*shall have been driving
you'll	have been driving	you	will have been driving
they'll	have been driving	they	will have been driving

ich werde nicht gefahren sein   −

I	won't/*shan't have been driving	I	will/*shall not have been driving
you	won't have been driving	you	will not have been driving
he	won't have been driving	he	will not have been driving
she	won't have been driving	she	will not have been driving
it	won't have been driving	it	will not have been driving
we	won't/*shan't have been driving	we	will/*shall not have been driving
you	won't have been driving	you	will not have been driving
they	won't have been driving	they	will not have been driving

Daneben sind auch die Kurzformen
I'll not have been driving, etc. gebräuchlich.

werde ich gefahren sein?   + ?

will/*shall	I	have been driving?
will	you	have been driving?
	he	have been driving?
	she	have been driving?
	it	have been driving?
will/*shall	we	have been driving?
will	you	have been driving?
	they	have been driving?

werde ich nicht gefahren sein?   − ?

won't/ *shan't	I	have been driving?	will/ *shall	I	not have been driving?
won't	you	have been driving?	will	you	not have been driving?
usw.			usw.		

35

present conditional continuous/future in the past continuous active

future in the past von **to be** + **present participle**

ich würde fahren

I'd	be driving	I	would/*should be driving
you'd	be driving	you	would be driving
he'd	be driving	he	would be driving
she'd	be driving	she	would be driving
it'd	be driving	it	would be driving
we'd	be driving	we	would/*should be driving
you'd	be driving	you	would be driving
they'd	be driving	they	would be driving

ich würde nicht fahren

I	wouldn't/*shouldn't be driving	I	would/*should not be driving
you	wouldn't be driving	you	would not be driving
he	wouldn't be driving	he	would not be driving
she	wouldn't be driving	she	would not be driving
it	wouldn't be driving	it	would not be driving
we	wouldn't/*shouldn't be driving	we	would/*should not be driving
you	wouldn't be driving	you	would not be driving
they	wouldn't be driving	they	would not be driving

Daneben sind auch die Kurzformen
I'd not be driving, etc. gebräuchlich.

würde ich fahren?

would/*should	I	be driving?
would	you	be driving?
	he	be driving?
	she	be driving?
	it	be driving?
would/*should	we	be driving?
would	you	be driving?
	they	be driving?

würde ich nicht fahren?

wouldn't/*shouldn't	I	be driving?	would/*should	I	not be driving?
wouldn't	you	be driving?	would	you	not be driving?
usw.			usw.		

perfect conditional continuous/future perfect in the past continuous active

future perfect in the past von **to be** + present participle

ich wäre gefahren

I'd	have been driving	I	would/*should have been driving
you'd	have been driving	you	would have been driving
he'd	have been driving	he	would have been driving
she'd	have been driving	she	would have been driving
it'd	have been driving	it	would have been driving
we'd	have been driving	we	would/*should have been driving
you'd	have been driving	you	would have been driving
they'd	have been driving	they	would have been driving

ich wäre nicht gefahren

I	wouldn't/*shouldn't have been driving	I	would/*should not have been driving
you	wouldn't have been driving	you	would not have been driving
he	wouldn't have been driving	he	would not have been driving
she	wouldn't have been driving	she	would not have been driving
it	wouldn't have been driving	it	would not have been driving
we	wouldn't/*shouldn't have been driving	we	would/*should not have been driving
you	wouldn't have been driving	you	would not have been driving
they	wouldn't have been driving	they	would not have been driving

Daneben sind auch die Kurzformen
I'd not have been driving, etc. gebräuchlich.

wäre ich gefahren?

would/*should	I	have been driving?
would	you	have been driving?
	he	have been driving?
	she	have been driving?
	it	have been driving?
would/*should	we	have been driving?
would	you	have been driving?
	they	have been driving?

wäre ich nicht gefahren?

wouldn't/ *shouldn't	I	have been driving?	would/ *should	I	not have been driving
wouldn't	you	have been driving?	would	you	not have been driving
usw.			usw.		

Vollverben

37

b) passive

present continuous passive

present von **to be** + **present participle passive**

ich werde gefahren   +

I'm	**being driven**	I	am	being driven
you're	being driven	you	are	being driven
he's	being driven	he	is	being driven
she's	being driven	she	is	being driven
it's	being driven	it	is	being driven
we're	being driven	we	are	being driven
you're	being driven	you	are	being driven
they're	being driven	they	are	being driven

ich werde nicht gefahren   –

I'm	not	being driven	I	am	not being driven
you	aren't	being driven	you	are	not being driven
he	isn't	being driven	he	is	not being driven
she	isn't	being driven	she	is	not being driven
it	isn't	being driven	it	is	not being driven
we	aren't	being driven	we	are	not being driven
you	aren't	being driven	you	are	not being driven
they	aren't	being driven	they	are	not being driven

Daneben sind auch die Kurzformen
you're not being driven, etc. gebräuchlich.

werde ich gefahren?   + ?

am	I	being driven?
are	you	being driven?
is	he	being driven?
	she	being driven?
	it	being driven?
are	we	being driven?
	you	being driven?
	they	being driven?

werde ich nicht gefahren?   – ?

aren't	I	being driven?	am	I	not being driven?
	you	being driven?	are	you	not being driven?
isn't	he	being driven?	is	he	not being driven?
	she	being driven?		she	not being driven?
	it	being driven?		it	not being driven?
aren't	we	being driven?	are	we	not being driven?
	you	being driven?		you	not being driven?
	they	being driven?		they	not being driven?

Vollverben (left margin)

past continuous passive

past von to be + present participle passive

ich wurde gefahren +

I	was	being driven
you	were	being driven
he	was	being driven
she	was	being driven
it	was	being driven
we	were	being driven
you	were	being driven
they	were	being driven

ich wurde nicht gefahren –

I	wasn't	being driven	I	was	not being driven
you	weren't	being driven	you	were	not being driven
he	wasn't	being driven	he	was	not being driven
she	wasn't	being driven	she	was	not being driven
it	wasn't	being driven	it	was	not being driven
we	weren't	being driven	we	were	not being driven
you	weren't	being driven	you	were	not being driven
they	weren't	being driven	they	were	not being driven

wurde ich gefahren? + ?

was	I	being driven?
were	you	being driven?
was	he	being driven?
	she	being driven?
	it	being driven?
were	we	being driven?
	you	being driven?
	they	being driven?

wurde ich nicht gefahren? – ?

wasn't	I	being driven?	was	I	not being driven?
weren't	you	being driven?	were	you	not being driven?
wasn't	he	being driven?	was	he	not being driven?
	she	being driven?		she	not being driven?
	it	being driven?		it	not being driven?
weren't	we	being driven?	were	we	not being driven?
	you	being driven?		you	not being driven?
	they	being driven?		they	not being driven?

Vollverben

	present	past	perfect
infinitive	**to be** sein		**to have been** gewesen sein
participle	**being** wörtl. „seiend"; wird am Satzanfang mit kausalem/temporalem Nebensatz übersetzt (da/während er/sie ... war)	**been** gewesen	**having been** wird im Deutschen meist mit kausalem/temporalem Nebensatz wiedergegeben (da/nachdem er/sie ... gewesen war)
gerund	**being** (das) Sein		**having been** häufiger wird auf die Form **gerund present** zurückgegriffen (vgl. S. 13)

imperative

bejahend	**be** sei!/seid!/seien Sie!
betont	**do be** sei/seid/seien Sie doch!
verneinend	**do not be/don't be** sei/seid/seien Sie nicht

present

ich bin

I'm	[aim]		I	am	[æm, əm]
you're	[juə]		you	are	[ɑ(ː)]
he's	[hiːz]		he	is	[iz]
she's	[ʃiːz]		she	is	[iz]
it's	[its]		it	is	[iz]
we're	[wiə]		we	are	[ɑ(ː)]
you're	[juə]		you	are	[ɑ(ː)]
they're	[ðeiə]		they	are	[ɑ(ː)]

ich bin nicht

I'm	not		I	am	not	
you	aren't	[ɑːnt]	you	are	not	
he	isn't	['iznt]	he	is	not	
she	isn't	['iznt]	she	is	not	
it	isn't	['iznt]	it	is	not	
we	aren't	[ɑːnt]	we	are	not	
you	aren't	[ɑːnt]	you	are	not	
they	aren't	[ɑːnt]	they	are	not	

Daneben sind auch die Kurzformen
you're not, etc. gebräuchlich.

bin ich?

am	I?
are	you?
is	he?
	she?
	it?
are	we?
	you?
	they?

bin ich nicht?

aren't	I?	am	I	not?
	you?	are	you	not?
isn't	he?	is	he	not?
	she?		she	not?
	it?		it	not?
aren't	we?	are	we	not?
	you?		you	not?
	they?		they	not?

Vollständige Hilfsverben

41

past

ich war

I	was	[wɔz, wəz]
you	were	[wə(ː)]
he	was	[wɔz, wəz]
she	was	[wɔz, wəz]
it	was	[wɔz, wəz]
we	were	[wə(ː)]
you	were	[wə(ː)]
they	were	[wə(ː)]

ich war nicht

I	wasn't	['wɔznt]	I	was	not
you	weren't	[wəːnt]	you	were	not
he	wasn't	['wɔznt]	he	was	not
she	wasn't	['wɔznt]	she	was	not
it	wasn't	['wɔznt]	it	was	not
we	weren't	[wəːnt]	we	were	not
you	weren't	[wəːnt]	you	were	not
they	weren't	[wəːnt]	they	were	not

war ich?

was	I?
were	you?
was	he?
	she?
	it?
were	we?
	you?
	they?

war ich nicht?

wasn't	I?	was	I	not?
weren't	you?	were	you	not?
wasn't	he?	was	he	not?
	she?		she	not?
	it?		it	not?
weren't	we?	were	we	not?
	you?		you	not?
	they?		they	not?

present von **to have** + **past participle**

ich bin gewesen/ich bin (seit)   +

I've	been		I	have	been
you've	been		you	have	been
he's	been		he	has	been
she's	been		she	has	been
it's	been		it	has	been
we've	been		we	have	been
you've	been		you	have	been
they've	been		they	have	been

ich bin nicht gewesen/ich bin (noch) nicht   –

I	haven't	been	I	have	not been
you	haven't	been	you	have	not been
he	hasn't	been	he	has	not been
she	hasn't	been	she	has	not been
it	hasn't	been	it	has	not been
we	haven't	been	we	have	not been
you	haven't	been	you	have	not been
they	haven't	been	they	have	not been

Daneben sind auch die Kurzformen
I've not been, etc. gebräuchlich.

bin ich (schon) gewesen?   + ?

have	I	been?
	you	been?
has	he	been?
	she	been?
	it	been?
have	we	been?
	you	been?
	they	been?

bin ich (noch) nicht gewesen?   – ?

haven't	I	been?	have	I	not been?
	you	been?		you	not been?
hasn't	he	been?	has	he	not been?
	she	been?		she	not been?
	it	been?		it	not been?
haven't	we	been?	have	we	not been?
	you	been?		you	not been?
	they	been?		they	not been?

Vollständige Hilfsverben

past perfect

past von **to have** + **past participle**

ich war gewesen   +

I'd	been	I	had been
you'd	been	you	had been
he'd	been	he	had been
she'd	been	she	had been
it'd	been	it	had been
we'd	been	we	had been
you'd	been	you	had been
they'd	been	they	had been

ich war nicht gewesen   –

I	hadn't been	I	had not been
you	hadn't been	you	had not been
he	hadn't been	he	had not been
she	hadn't been	she	had not been
it	hadn't been	it	had not been
we	hadn't been	we	had not been
you	hadn't been	you	had not been
they	hadn't been	they	had not been

Daneben sind auch die Kurzformen
I'd not been, etc. gebräuchlich.

war ich gewesen?   + ?

had	I	been?
	you	been?
	he	been?
	she	been?
	it	been?
	we	been?
	you	been?
	they	been?

war ich nicht gewesen?   – ?

hadn't	I	been?	had	I	not been?
	you	been?		you	not been?
	he	been?		he	not been?
	she	been?		she	not been?
	it	been?		it	not been?
	we	been?		we	not been?
	you	been?		you	not been?
	they	been?		they	not been?

future

will/*shall + infinitive

ich werde sein   +

I'll	be	I	will/*shall be
you'll	be	you	will be
he'll	be	he	will be
she'll	be	she	will be
it'll	be	it	will be
we'll	be	we	will/*shall be
you'll	be	you	will be
they'll	be	they	will be

ich werde nicht sein   –

I	won't/*shan't be	I	will/*shall not be
you	won't be	you	will not be
he	won't be	he	will not be
she	won't be	she	will not be
it	won't be	it	will not be
we	won't/*shan't be	we	will/*shall not be
you	won't be	you	will not be
they	won't be	they	will not be

Daneben sind auch die Kurzformen
I'll not be, etc. gebräuchlich.

werde ich sein?   + ?

will/*shall	I	be?
will	you	be?
	he	be?
	she	be?
	it	be?
will/*shall	we	be?
will	you	be?
	they	be?

werde ich nicht sein?   – ?

won't/ *shan't	I	be?	will/ *shall	I	not be?
won't	you	be?	will	you	not be?
usw.			usw.		

Anstatt mit „will" + infinitive kann das **future** auch mit „to be going to"
+ infinitive gebildet werden. Dabei wird nur das Hilfsverb „to be" entsprechend konjugiert.

future perfect

will/*shall + perfect infinitive

ich werde gewesen sein

I'll	have been	I	will/*shall have been
you'll	have been	you	will have been
he'll	have been	he	will have been
she'll	have been	she	will have been
it'll	have been	it	will have been
we'll	have been	we	will/*shall have been
you'll	have been	you	will have been
they'll	have been	they	will have been

ich werde nicht gewesen sein

I	won't/*shan't have been	I	will/*shall not have been
you	won't have been	you	will not have been
he	won't have been	he	will not have been
she	won't have been	she	will not have been
it	won't have been	it	will not have been
we	won't/*shan't have been	we	will/*shall not have been
you	won't have been	you	will not have been
they	won't have been	they	will not have been

Daneben sind auch die Kurzformen
I'll not have been, etc. gebräuchlich.

werde ich gewesen sein?

will/*shall	I	have been?
will	you	have been?
	he	have been?
	she	have been?
	it	have been?
will/*shall	we	have been?
will	you	have been?
	they	have been?

werde ich nicht gewesen sein?

won't/*shan't	I	have been?	will/*shall	I	not have been?
won't	you	have been?	will	you	not have been?
	he	have been?		he	not have been?
	she	have been?		she	not have been?
	it	have been?		it	not have been?
won't/*shan't	we	have been?	will/*shall	we	not have been?
won't	you	have been?	will	you	not have been?
	they	have been?		they	not have been?

present conditional/future in the past

would/*should + infinitive

ich wäre   +

I'd	be	I	would/*should be
you'd	be	you	would be
he'd	be	he	would be
she'd	be	she	would be
it'd	be	it	would be
we'd	be	we	would/*should be
you'd	be	you	would be
they'd	be	they	would be

ich wäre nicht   –

I	wouldn't/*shouldn't be	I	would/*should not be
you	wouldn't be	you	would not be
he	wouldn't be	he	would not be
she	wouldn't be	she	would not be
it	wouldn't be	it	would not be
we	wouldn't/*shouldn't be	we	would/*should not be
you	wouldn't be	you	would not be
they	wouldn't be	they	would not be

Daneben sind auch die Kurzformen
I'd not be, etc. gebräuchlich.

wäre ich?   + ?

would/*should	I	be?
would	you	be?
	he	be?
	she	be?
	it	be?
would/*should	we	be?
would	you	be?
	they	be?

wäre ich nicht?   – ?

wouldn't/	I	be?	would/	I	not be?
*shouldn't			*should		
wouldn't	you	be?	would	you	not be?
usw.			usw.		

Anstatt mit „**would**" + **infinitive** kann das **future in the past** (nicht das
present conditional!) auch mit „**was/were going to**" + **infinitive** gebildet
werden. Dabei wird nur das Hilfsverb „**to be**" entsprechend konjugiert.

perfect conditional/future perfect in the past

would/*should + perfect infinitive

ich wäre gewesen

I'd	have been	I	would/*should have been
you'd	have been	you	would have been
he'd	have been	he	would have been
she'd	have been	she	would have been
it'd	have been	it	would have been
we'd	have been	we	would/*should have been
you'd	have been	you	would have been
they'd	have been	they	would have been

ich wäre nicht gewesen

I	wouldn't/*shouldn't have been	I	would/*should not have been
you	wouldn't have been	you	would not have been
he	wouldn't have been	he	would not have been
she	wouldn't have been	she	would not have been
it	wouldn't have been	it	would not have been
we	wouldn't/*shouldn't have been	we	would/*should not have been
you	wouldn't have been	you	would not have been
they	wouldn't have been	they	would not have been

Daneben sind auch die Kurzformen
I'd not have been, etc. gebräuchlich.

wäre ich gewesen?

would/*should	I	have been?
would	you	have been?
	he	have been?
	she	have been?
	it	have been?
would/*should	we	have been?
would	you	have been?
	they	have been?

wäre ich nicht gewesen?

wouldn't/ *shouldn't	I	have been?	would/ *should	I	not have been?
wouldn't	you	have been?	would	you	not have been
usw.			usw.		

2. to have

Als Vollverb bildet „to have" die Formen für Frage und Verneinung auch wie „to drive".

	present	past	perfect
infinitive	**to have** haben		**to have had** gehabt haben
participle	**having** wörtl. „habend"; wird am Satzanfang mit kausalem/temporalem Nebensatz übersetzt (da/während er/sie … hatte)	**had** gehabt	**having had** wird im Deutschen meist mit kausalem/temporalem Nebensatz wiedergegeben (da/nachdem er/sie … gehabt hatten)
gerund	**having** (das) Haben		**having had** häufiger wird auf die Form **gerund present** zurückgegriffen

imperative

bejahend	**have** hab(e)!/habt!/haben Sie!
betont	**do have** hab(e)/habt/haben Sie doch!
verneinend	**do not have/don't have** hab(e)/habt/haben Sie nicht!

Vollständige Hilfsverben

present

ich habe

+

I've	[aiv]		I	have	[hæv, həv]
you've	[ju:v]		you	have	[hæv, həv]
he's	[hi:z]		he	has	[hæz, həz]
she's	[ʃi:z]		she	has	[hæz, həz]
it's	[its]		it	has	[hæz, həz]
we've	[wi:v]		we	have	[hæv, həv]
you've	[ju:v]		you	have	[hæv, həv]
they've	[ðeiv]		they	have	[hæv, həv]

ich habe nicht

—

I	haven't	['hævnt]		I	have	not
you	haven't	['hævnt]		you	have	not
he	hasn't	['hæznt]		he	has	not
she	hasn't	['hæznt]		she	has	not
it	hasn't	['hæznt]		it	has	not
we	haven't	['hævnt]		we	have	not
you	haven't	['hævnt]		you	have	not
they	haven't	['hævnt]		they	have	not

Daneben sind auch die Kurzformen
I've not, etc. gebräuchlich.

habe ich?

+ ?

have	I?
	you?
has	he?
	she?
	it?
have	we?
	you?
	they?

habe ich nicht?

− ?

haven't	I?		have	I	not?
	you?			you	not?
hasn't	he?		has	he	not?
	she?			she	not?
	it?			it	not?
haven't	we?		have	we	not?
	you?			you	not?
	they?			they	not?

past

ich hatte +

I'd	[aid]	I	had	[hæd, həd]
you'd	[juːd]	you	had	
he'd	[hiːd]	he	had	
she'd	[ʃiːd]	she	had	
it'd	['itəd]	it	had	
we'd	[wiːd]	we	had	
you'd	[juːd]	you	had	
they'd	[ðeid]	they	had	

ich hatte nicht −

I	hadn't	['hædnt]	I	had not
you	hadn't		you	had not
he	hadn't		he	had not
she	hadn't		she	had not
it	hadn't		it	had not
we	hadn't		we	had not
you	hadn't		you	had not
they	hadn't		they	had not

hatte ich? + ?

had	I?
	you?
	he?
	she?
	it?
	we?
	you?
	they?

hatte ich nicht? − ?

hadn't	I?	had	I	not?
	you?		you	not?
	he?		he	not?
	she?		she	not?
	it?		it	not?
	we?		we	not?
	you?		you	not?
	they?		they	not?

Vollständige Hilfsverben

present perfect

present von **to have** + **past participle**

ich habe gehabt/ich habe (seit)   +

I've	had		I	have	had
you've	had		you	have	had
he's	had		he	has	had
she's	had		she	has	had
it's	had		it	has	had
we've	had		we	have	had
you've	had		you	have	had
they've	had		they	have	had

ich habe (noch) nicht gehabt   −

I	haven't	had		I	have	not had
you	haven't	had		you	have	not had
he	hasn't	had		he	has	not had
she	hasn't	had		she	has	not had
it	hasn't	had		it	has	not had
we	haven't	had		we	have	not had
you	haven't	had		you	have	not had
they	haven't	had		they	have	not had

Daneben sind auch die Kurzformen
I've not had, etc. gebräuchlich.

habe ich (schon) gehabt?   + ?

have	I	had?
	you	had?
	he	had?
	she	had?
	it	had?
	we	had?
	you	had?
	they	had?

habe ich (noch) nicht gehabt?   − ?

haven't	I	had?	have	I	not had?
	you	had?		you	not had?
	he	had?		he	not had?
	she	had?		she	not had?
	it	had?		it	not had?
	we	had?		we	not had?
	you	had?		you	not had?
	they	had?		they	not had?

Vollständige Hilfsverben

past perfect

past von **to have** + **past participle**

ich hatte gehabt   +

I'd	had		I	had had
you'd	had		you	had had
he'd	had		he	had had
she'd	had		she	had had
it'd	had		it	had had
we'd	had		we	had had
you'd	had		you	had had
they'd	had		they	had had

ich hatte nicht gehabt   –

I	hadn't had		I	had not had
you	hadn't had		you	had not had
he	hadn't had		he	had not had
she	hadn't had		she	had not had
it	hadn't had		it	had not had
we	hadn't had		we	had not had
you	hadn't had		you	had not had
they	hadn't had		they	had not had

Daneben sind auch die Kurzformen
I'd not had, etc. gebräuchlich.

hatte ich gehabt?   + ?

had	I	had?
	you	had?
	he	had?
	she	had?
	it	had?
	we	had?
	you	had?
	they	had?

hatte ich nicht gehabt?   – ?

hadn't	I	had?	had	I	not had?
	you	had?		you	not had?
	he	had?		he	not had?
	she	had?		she	not had?
	it	had?		it	not had?
	we	had?		we	not had?
	you	had?		you	not had?
	they	had?		they	not had?

future

will/*shall + infinitive

ich werde haben

I'll	have		I	will/*shall have
you'll	have		you	will have
he'll	have		he	will have
she'll	have		she	will have
it'll	have		it	will have
we'll	have		we	will/*shall have
you'll	have		you	will have
they'll	have		they	will have

ich werde nicht haben

I	won't/*shan't have		I	will/*shall not have
you	won't have		you	will not have
he	won't have		he	will not have
she	won't have		she	will not have
it	won't have		it	will not have
we	won't/*shan't have		we	will/*shall not have
you	won't have		you	will not have
they	won't have		they	will not have

Daneben sind auch die Kurzformen
I'll not have, etc. gebräuchlich.

werde ich haben?

will/*shall	I	have?
will	you	have?
	he	have?
	she	have?
	it	have?
will/*shall	we	have?
will	you	have?
	they	have?

werde ich nicht haben?

won't/ *shan't	I	have?		will/ *shall	I	not have?
won't	you	have?		will	you	not have?
usw.				usw.		

Anstatt mit „will" + **infinitive** kann das **future** auch mit „to be going to"
+ **infinitive** gebildet werden. Dabei wird nur das Hilfsverb „to be" (siehe
dort) entsprechend konjugiert.

future perfect

will/*shall + perfect infinitive

ich werde gehabt haben   **+**

I'll	have had	I	will/*shall have had
you'll	have had	you	will have had
he'll	have had	he	will have had
she'll	have had	she	will have had
it'll	have had	it	will have had
we'll	have had	we	will/*shall have had
you'll	have had	you	will have had
they'll	have had	they	will have had

ich werde nicht gehabt haben   **−**

I	won't/*shan't have had	I	will/*shall not have had
you	won't have had	you	will not have had
he	won't have had	he	will not have had
she	won't have had	she	will not have had
it	won't have had	it	will not have had
we	won't/*shan't have had	we	will/*shall not have had
you	won't have had	you	will not have had
they	won't have had	they	will not have had

Daneben sind auch die Kurzformen
I'll not have had, etc. gebräuchlich.

werde ich gehabt haben?   **+ ?**

will/*shall	I	have had?
will	you	have had?
	he	have had?
	she	have had?
	it	have had?
will/*shall	we	have had?
	you	have had?
	they	have had?

werde ich nicht gehabt haben?   **− ?**

won't/*shan't	I	have had?	will/*shall	I	not have had?
won't	you	have had?	will	you	not have had?
	he	have had?		he	not have had?
	she	have had?		she	not have had?
	it	have had?		it	not have had?
won't/*shan't	we	have had?	will/*shall	we	not have had?
won't	you	have had?	will	you	not have had?
	they	have had?		they	not have had?

Vollständige Hilfsverben

present conditional/future in the past

would/*should + infinitive

ich hätte

I'd	have	I	would/*should have
you'd	have	you	would have
he'd	have	he	would have
she'd	have	she	would have
it'd	have	it	would have
we'd	have	we	would/*should have
you'd	have	you	would have
they'd	have	they	would have

ich hätte nicht

I	wouldn't/*shouldn't have	I	would/*should not have
you	wouldn't have	you	would not have
he	wouldn't have	he	would not have
she	wouldn't have	she	would not have
it	wouldn't have	it	would not have
we	wouldn't/*shouldn't have	we	would/*should not have
you	wouldn't have	you	would not have
they	wouldn't have	they	would not have

Daneben sind auch die Kurzformen
I'd not have, etc. gebräuchlich.

hätte ich?

would/*should	I	have?
would	you	have?
	he	have?
	she	have?
	it	have?
would/*should	we	have?
would	you	have?
	they	have?

hätte ich nicht?

wouldn't/ *shouldn't	I	have?		would/ *should	I	not have?
wouldn't	you	have?		would	you	not have?
usw.				usw.		

Anstatt mit „would" + **infinitive** kann das **future in the past** (nicht das
present conditional!) auch mit „was/were going to" + **infinitive** gebildet
werden. Dabei wird nur das Hilfsverb „was/were" (siehe „to be") entsprechend konjugiert.

perfect conditional/future perfect in the past

would/*should + perfect infinitive

ich hätte gehabt   +

I'd	have had	I	would/*should have had
you'd	have had	you	would have had
he'd	have had	he	would have had
she'd	have had	she	would have had
it'd	have had	it	would have had
we'd	have had	we	would/*should have had
you'd	have had	you	would have had
they'd	have had	they	would have had

ich hätte nicht gehabt   −

I	wouldn't/*shouldn't have had	I	would/*should not have had
you	wouldn't have had	you	would not have had
he	wouldn't have had	he	would not have had
she	wouldn't have had	she	would not have had
it	wouldn't have had	it	would not have had
we	wouldn't/*shouldn't have had	we	would/*should not have had
you	wouldn't have had	you	would not have had
they	wouldn't have had	they	would not have had

Daneben sind auch die Kurzformen
I'd not have had, etc. gebräuchlich.

hätte ich gehabt?   + ?

would/*should	I	have had?
would	you	have had?
	he	have had?
	she	have had?
	it	have had?
would/*should	we	have had?
would	you	have had?
	they	have had?

hätte ich nicht gehabt?   − ?

wouldn't/ *shouldn't	I	have had?	would/ *should	I	not have had?
wouldn't	you	have had?	would	you	not have had?
usw.			usw.		

3. to do

Als **Hilfsverb** (zur Umschreibung bei Frage und Verneinung mit **not** und zur Hervorhebung) bildet **to do** nur **present** und **past**.

Als **Vollverb** (in der Bedeutung „tun", „machen", „erledigen" usw.) bildet **to do** auch **alle** übrigen **Zeiten** wie andere Vollverben.

	present	past	perfect
infinitive	**to do** tun		**to have done** getan haben
participle	**doing** wörtl. „tuend"; wird am Satzanfang mit kausalem/temporalem Nebensatz übersetzt (da/während er/sie … tat)	**done** [dʌn] getan	**having done** wird im Deutschen meist mit kausalem/temporalem Nebensatz wiedergegeben (da/nachdem er/sie … getan hatte)
gerund	**doing** (das) Tun		**having done** häufiger wird auf die Form **gerund present** zurückgegriffen

imperative

bejahend	**do** tu!/tut!/tun Sie!
betont	**do do** tu/tut/tun Sie doch!
verneinend	**do not do/don't do** tu/tut/tun Sie nicht!

Vollständige Hilfsverben

present

ich tue

I	**do**	[du(ː)]
you	**do**	[du(ː)]
he	**does**	[dʌz, dəz]
she	**does**	[dʌz, dəz]
it	**does**	[dʌz, dəz]
we	**do**	[du(ː)]
you	**do**	[du(ː)]
they	**do**	[du(ː)]

ich tue nicht

I	**don't**	[dəunt]	I	**do**	**not**
you	**don't**	[dəunt]	you	**do**	**not**
he	**doesn't**	['dʌznt]	he	**does**	**not**
she	**doesn't**	['dʌznt]	she	**does**	**not**
it	**doesn't**	['dʌznt]	it	**does**	**not**
we	**don't**	[dəunt]	we	**do**	**not**
you	**don't**	[dəunt]	you	**do**	**not**
they	**don't**	[dəunt]	they	**do**	**not**

tue ich?

do	**I?**
	you?
does	**he?**
	she?
	it?
do	**we?**
	you?
	they?

tue ich nicht?

don't	**I?**	**do**	**I**	**not?**
	you?		**you**	**not?**
doesn't	**he?**	**does**	**he**	**not?**
	she?		**she**	**not?**
	it?		**it**	**not?**
don't	**we?**	**do**	**we**	**not?**
	you?		**you**	**not?**
	they?		**they**	**not?**

Vollständige Hilfsverben

past

ich tat

I	**did** [did]
you	**did**
he	**did**
she	**did**
it	**did**
we	**did**
you	**did**
they	**did**

ich tat nicht

I	**didn't** ['didnt]	I	**did not**
you	**didn't**	you	**did not**
he	**didn't**	he	**did not**
she	**didn't**	she	**did not**
it	**didn't**	it	**did not**
we	**didn't**	we	**did not**
you	**didn't**	you	**did not**
they	**didn't**	they	**did not**

tat ich?

did	**I?**
	you?
	he?
	she?
	it?
	we?
	you?
	they?

tat ich nicht?

didn't	**I?**	**did**	**I**	**not?**
	you?		**you**	**not?**
	he?		**he**	**not?**
	she?		**she**	**not?**
	it?		**it**	**not?**
	we?		**we**	**not?**
	you?		**you**	**not?**
	they?		**they**	**not?**

Vollständige Hilfsverben

Unvollständige (modale) Hilfsverben
1. can – could

Grundbedeutung:	Fähigkeit	Möglichkeit	Erlaubnis
Ersatzverben zur Umschreibung der fehlenden Zeitformen	**to be able to** fähig/in der Lage sein zu (tun), können	**it is possible to** es ist möglich zu (tun), man kann	**to be allowed to, to be permitted to,** die Erlaubnis haben zu (tun), dürfen

present

ich kann   +

I	**can** [kæn, kən]
you	**can**
he	**can**
she	**can**
it	**can**
we	**can**
you	**can**
they	**can**

ich kann nicht   –

I	**can't** [kɑːnt, kænt]		I	**cannot** [ˈkænɔt]
you	**can't**		you	**cannot**
he	**can't**		he	**cannot**
she	**can't**		she	**cannot**
it	**can't**		it	**cannot**
we	**can't**		we	**cannot**
you	**can't**		you	**cannot**
they	**can't**		they	**cannot**

kann ich?   + ?

can	**I?**
usw.	

kann ich nicht?   – ?

can't	**I?**		**can**	**I**	**not?**
usw.			usw.		

past

ich konnte/könnte

I	**could** [kud, kəd]
you	could
he	could
she	could
it	could
we	could
you	could
they	could

ich konnte/könnte nicht

I	**couldn't** ['kudnt]	I	could not
you	couldn't	you	could not
he	couldn't	he	could not
she	couldn't	she	could not
it	couldn't	it	could not
we	couldn't	we	could not
you	couldn't	you	could not
they	couldn't	they	could not

konnte/könnte ich?

could	**I?**
	you?
	he?
	she?
	it?
	we?
	you?
	they?

konnte/könnte ich nicht?

couldn't I?		**could**	**I**	**not?**
you?			you	not?
he?			he	not?
she?			she	not?
it?			it	not?
we?			we	not?
you?			you	not?
they?			they	not?

Unvollständige Hilfsverben

2. may – might

Grundbedeutung:	Erlaubnis	Möglichkeit
Ersatzverben zur Umschreibung der fehlenden Zeitformen	**to be allowed to, to be permitted to** die Erlaubnis haben zu (tun), dürfen	**it is possible that** es ist möglich, dass ...; vielleicht ...
Verneinung	**may not, must not, cannot** oder Verneinung der entsprechenden Ersatzverben	**cannot**

present

ich darf   +

I	**may** [mei]
you	**may**
he	**may**
she	**may**
it	**may**
we	**may**
you	**may**
they	**may**

ich darf nicht   –

*I	**mayn't** ['meint]	I	**may not**
*you	**mayn't**	you	**may not**
*he	**mayn't**	he	**may not**
*she	**mayn't**	she	**may not**
*it	**mayn't**	it	**may not**
*we	**mayn't**	we	**may not**
*you	**mayn't**	you	**may not**
*they	**mayn't**	they	**may not**

darf ich?   + ?

may	**I?**
usw.	

darf ich nicht?   – ?

*****mayn't I?**		**may**	**I**	**not?**
usw.		usw.	

Unvollständige Hilfsverben

past

ich dürfte (seltener: ich durfte) +

I	**might** [mait]
you	**might**
he	**might**
she	**might**
it	**might**
we	**might**
you	**might**
they	**might**

ich dürfte nicht (seltener: ich durfte nicht) —

I	**mightn't** ['maitnt]		I	**might not**
you	**mightn't**		you	**might not**
he	**mightn't**		he	**might not**
she	**mightn't**		she	**might not**
it	**mightn't**		it	**might not**
we	**mightn't**		we	**might not**
you	**mightn't**		you	**might not**
they	**mightn't**		they	**might not**

dürfte ich? (seltener: durfte ich?) + ?

might	**I?**
	you?
	he?
	she?
	it?
	we?
	you?
	they?

dürfte ich nicht? (seltener: durfte ich nicht?) — ?

mightn't	**I?**		**might**	**I**	**not?**
	you?			**you**	**not?**
	he?			**he**	**not?**
	she?			**she**	**not?**
	it?			**it**	**not?**
	we?			**we**	**not?**
	you?			**you**	**not?**
	they?			**they**	**not?**

Unvollständige Hilfsverben

3. must (– must)

Grundbedeutung:	**Zwang, Verpflichtung, Notwendigkeit**	
	vom Sprecher ausgehend	von äußeren Umständen ausgehend
	must muss(t), müsst, müssen (im Past nur in abhängigen Sätzen)	**to have (got) to** müssen
Ersatzverben zur Umschreibung der fehlenden Zeitformen	**to have (got) to** müssen **to be obliged to** verpflichtet sein zu (tun), müssen **to be forced/compelled to** gezwungen sein zu (tun), müssen	
Verneinung der	**Notwendigkeit** nicht (zu tun) brauchen	**Erlaubnis (= Verbot)** nicht (tun) dürfen
	need not **have not (got) to** **do not have to**	**must not** **to be not to** **to be not allowed/ permitted to**

present

ich muss   +

I	**must** [mʌst, məst]		
usw.			

ich darf nicht

I	**mustn't** ['mʌsnt]	**I**	**must not**
usw.		usw.	

muss ich?   + ?

must	**I?**	
usw.		

muss ich nicht?   – ?

mustn't I?		**must**	**I** **not?**
usw.		usw.	

past (nur in abhängigen Sätzen) = **present**

Unvollständige Hilfsverben

4. shall – should

Grundbedeutung:	in der **1. Person**		in der **1.**, **2.** und **3. Person**	
	*shall	*should	shall	should
	werde(n)	würde(n)	**Anordnung:**	**Pflicht, Rat:**
	zur Bildung des		soll(st),	sollte(st),
	future	**conditional**	sollt, sollen	sollte,
				sollten

Anordnung eines Dritten	to be to sollen

Ersatzverb	to be to sollen

present

ich soll (1. Person auch: ich werde)   +

I	shall [ʃæl, ʃəl]
you	shall
he	shall
she	shall
it	shall
we	shall
you	shall
they	shall

ich soll nicht (1. Person auch: ich werde nicht)   −

I	shan't [ʃɑːnt]	I	shall not
you	shan't	you	shall not
he	shan't	he	shall not
she	shan't	she	shall not
it	shan't	it	shall not
we	shan't	we	shall not
you	shan't	you	shall not
they	shan't	they	shall not

soll ich? (1. Person auch: werde ich?)   + ?

shall	I?
usw.	

soll ich nicht? (1. Person auch: werde ich nicht?)   − ?

shan't	I?	shall	I	not?
usw.		usw.		

past

ich sollte (1. Person auch: ich würde) +

I	should [ʃud, ʃəd]
you	should
he	should
she	should
it	should
we	should
you	should
they	should

ich sollte nicht (1. Person auch: ich würde nicht) —

I	shouldn't ['ʃudnt]		I	should not
you	shouldn't		you	should not
he	shouldn't		he	should not
she	shouldn't		she	should not
it	shouldn't		it	should not
we	shouldn't		we	should not
you	shouldn't		you	should not
they	shouldn't		they	should not

sollte ich? (1. Person auch: würde ich?) + ?

should	I?
	you?
	he?
	she?
	it?
	we?
	you?
	they?

sollte ich nicht? (1. Person auch: würde ich nicht?) − ?

shouldn't	I?		should	I	not?
	you?			you	not?
	he?			he	not?
	she?			she	not?
	it?			it	not?
	we?			we	not?
	you?			you	not?
	they?			they	not?

Unvollständige Hilfsverben

5. will – would

Grundbedeutung:	will werde(n)	would würde(n)	Wille, Absicht
	zur Bildung des		will(st), wollt,
	future	**conditional**	wollen
	allgemeine Wahrheit (es ist immer so)	**Gewohnheit** zu (tun) pflegen, (etwas) immer (tun)	

Ersatzverben	**to wish/want to** wünschen zu (tun)
zum Ausdruck	**to like to** gern (tun) mögen
des Willens,	**to intend to** beabsichtigen zu (tun)
der Absicht	**to be willing to** bereit sein zu (tun)

present

ich werde (seltener: ich will)   +

I'll	[ail]		I	will [wil]
you'll	[ju:l]		you	will
he'll	[hi:l]		he	will
she'll	[ʃi:l]		she	will
it'll	['itl]		it	will
we'll	[wi:l]		we	will
you'll	[ju:l]		you	will
they'll	[ðeil]		they	will

ich werde nicht (seltener: ich will nicht)   –

I	won't [wəunt]		I	will not
you	**won't**		you	will not
he	**won't**		he	will not
she	**won't**		she	will not
it	**won't**		it	will not
we	**won't**		we	will not
you	**won't**		you	will not
they	**won't**		they	will not

Daneben sind auch die Kurzformen
I'll not, etc. gebräuchlich.

werde ich? (seltener: will ich?)   +?

will	**I?**
usw.	

werde ich nicht? (seltener: will ich nicht?)   –?

won't	**I?**		**will**	**I**	**not?**
usw.			usw.		

68

past

ich würde (seltener: ich wollte)   +

I'd	[aid]		I	would [wud, wəd]
you'd	[ju:d]		you	would
he'd	[hi:d]		he	would
she'd	[ʃi:d]		she	would
it'd	['it:d]		it	would
we'd	[wi:d]		we	would
you'd	[ju:d]		you	would
they'd	[ðeid]		they	would

ich würde nicht (seltener: ich wollte nicht)   –

I	wouldn't ['wudnt]		I	would not
you	wouldn't		you	would not
he	wouldn't		he	would not
she	wouldn't		she	would not
it	wouldn't		it	would not
we	wouldn't		we	would not
you	wouldn't		you	would not
they	wouldn't		they	would not

Daneben sind auch die Kurzformen
I'd not, etc. gebräuchlich.

würde ich? (seltener: wollte ich?)   + ?

would	I?
	you?
	he?
	she?
	it?
	we?
	you?
	they?

würde ich nicht? (seltener: wollte ich nicht?)   – ?

wouldn't	I?		would	I	not?
	you?			you	not?
	he?			he	not?
	she?			she	not?
	it?			it	not?
	we?			we	not?
	you?			you	not?
	they?			they	not?

Unvollständige Hilfsverben

6. used to

Bedeutung	**Gewohnheit** in der Vergangenheit
Formen	**I used to smoke** (früher) rauchte ich = war ich Raucher
Gebrauch	nur **past**

past

ich pflegte zu …   +

I	used to [ˈjuːstə]
you	used to
he	used to
she	used to
it	used to
we	used to
you	used to
they	used to

ich pflegte nicht zu …   –

*I	usedn't to		I	used not to
*you	usedn't to		you	used not to
*he	usedn't to		he	used not to
*she	usedn't to		she	used not to
*it	usedn't to		it	used not to
*we	usedn't to		we	used not to
*you	usedn't to		you	used not to
*they	usedn't to		they	used not to

Daneben sind auch die Kurzformen
I didn't use to[1], etc. gebräuchlich.

pflegte ich zu …?   + ?

*used	I	to?		did	I	use to?[1]
usw.				usw.		

pflegte ich nicht zu …?   – ?

*usedn't	I	to?		used	I	not to?
usw.				usw.		

Daneben sind auch die Kurzformen
didn't I use to[1], etc. gebräuchlich.

---

1 obwohl „**used to**" streng genommen nur im **past tense** existiert, findet
man diese Form häufig

7. ought to

Grundbedeutung: **sittliche Verpflichtung** ich sollte (eigentlich)
(auf Gegenwart oder Zukunft bezogen)

ich sollte (eigentlich)   +

I	**ought to** [ˈɔːtə]
you	**ought to**
he	**ought to**
she	**ought to**
it	**ought to**
we	**ought to**
you	**ought to**
they	**ought to**

ich sollte (eigentlich) nicht   −

I	**oughtn't to** [ˈɔːtnt]		I	**ought not to**
you	**oughtn't to**		you	**ought not to**
he	**oughtn't to**		he	**ought not to**
she	**oughtn't to**		she	**ought not to**
it	**oughtn't to**		it	**ought not to**
we	**oughtn't to**		we	**ought not to**
you	**oughtn't to**		you	**ought not to**
they	**oughtn't to**		they	**ought not to**

sollte ich (eigentlich)?   + ?

ought	**I**	**to?**
	you	**to?**
	he	**to?**
	she	**to?**
	it	**to?**
	we	**to?**
	you	**to?**
	they	**to?**

sollte ich (eigentlich) nicht?   − ?

oughtn't	**I**	**to?**		**ought**	**I**	**not to?**
	you	**to?**			**you**	**not to?**
	he	**to?**			**he**	**not to?**
	she	**to?**			**she**	**not to?**
	it	**to?**			**it**	**not to?**
	we	**to?**			**we**	**not to?**
	you	**to?**			**you**	**not to?**
	they	**to?**			**they**	**not to?**

Unvollständige Hilfsverben

8. to need – needed/to dare – dared

Need und **dare** können sowohl als Hilfsverb wie auch als Vollverb verwendet werden.

to need – needed

	Bedeutung	Formen, Gebrauch
Vollverb	benötigen	wie regelmäßiges Vollverb **He needs the book**
Hilfsverb	zu (tun) brauchen	wie unvollständiges Hilfsverb, sehr selten in der bejahten Form **He need not come**

to dare – dared

	Bedeutung	Formen, Gebrauch
Vollverb	zu (tun) wagen	wie regelmäßiges Vollverb **He dares to answer**
Hilfsverb		wie unvollständiges Hilfsverb, bejahte Form jedoch nur in der Frage **How dare he do that?** **She dare not answer**

Listen unregelmäßiger Verben
1. Übersicht über die Stammformen

Mit Stern (*) gekennzeichnete Formen können auch durch die regelmäßig
gebildete Form auf **-ed** ersetzt werden.

infinitive	past	past participle	
abide [ai]	abode* [əu]	abode* [əu]	bleiben
arise [ai]	arose [əu]	arisen [i]	sich erheben
awake [ei]	awoke [əu]	awoken [əu]	erwachen
be [i(ː)]	was [ɔ, ə], were [ə(ː)]	been [i(ː)]	sein
bear [ɛə]	bore [ɔ]	borne [ɔː] born [ɔː]	(er)tragen; geboren
beat [iː]	beat [iː]	beaten [iː]	schlagen
become [ʌ]	became [ei]	become [ʌ]	werden
beget [e]	begot [ɔ]	begotten [ɔ]	zeugen
begin [i]	began [æ]	begun [ʌ]	anfangen
bend [e]	bent [e]	bent [e]	beugen
beseech [iː]	besought* [ɔː]	besought* [ɔː]	ersuchen
bet [e]	bet* [e]	bet* [e]	wetten
bid [i]	bade [ei], bid [i]	bidden [i], bid [i]	befehlen bieten
bide [ai]	bode* [əu]	bided [ai]	abwarten
bind [ai]	bound [au]	bound [au]	binden
bite [ai]	bit [i]	bitten [i]	beißen
bleed [iː]	bled [e]	bled [e]	bluten
blow [əu]	blew [uː]	blown [əu]	blasen; blühen
break [ei]	broke [əu]	broken [əu]	brechen
breed [iː]	bred [e]	bred [e]	aufziehen
bring [i]	brought [ɔː]	brought [ɔː]	bringen
build [i]	built [i]	built [i]	bauen
burn [əː]	burnt* [əː]	burnt* [əː]	brennen
burst [əː]	burst [əː]	burst [əː]	bersten
buy [ai]	bought [ɔː]	bought [ɔː]	kaufen
cast [ɑː]	cast [ɑː]	cast [ɑː]	werfen
catch [æ]	caught [ɔː]	caught [ɔː]	fangen
chide [ai]	chid* [i]	chid(den)* [i]	schelten
choose [uː]	chose [əu]	chosen [əu]	wählen
cleave [iː]	cleft [e], clove* [əu]	cleft [e], cloven* [əu]	(sich) spalten
cling [i]	clung [ʌ]	clung [ʌ]	sich (an)klammern
come [ʌ]	came [ei]	come [ʌ]	kommen
cost [ɔ]	cost [ɔ]	cost [ɔ]	kosten
creep [iː]	crept [e]	crept [e]	kriechen
cut [ʌ]	cut [ʌ]	cut [ʌ]	schneiden

infinitive	past	past participle	
deal [i:]	dealt [e]	dealt [e]	handeln
dig [i]	dug [ʌ]	dug [ʌ]	graben
do [u(:)]	did [i]	done [ʌ]	tun
draw [ɔ:]	drew [u:]	drawn [ɔ:]	ziehen; zeichnen
dream [i:]	dreamt* [e]	dreamt* [e]	träumen
drink [i:]	drank [æ]	drunk [ʌ]	trinken
drive [ai]	drove [əu]	driven [i]	treiben; fahren
dwell [e]	dwelt* [e]	dwelt* [e]	wohnen
eat [i:]	ate [e]	eaten [i:]	essen
fall [ɔ:]	fell [e]	fallen [ɔ:]	fallen
feed [i:]	fed [e]	fed [e]	füttern
feel [i:]	felt [e]	felt [e]	fühlen
fight [ai]	fought [ɔ:]	fought [ɔ:]	kämpfen
find [ai]	found [au]	found [au]	finden
flee [i:]	fled [e]	fled [e]	fliehen
fling [i]	flung [ʌ]	flung [ʌ]	schleudern
fly [ai]	flew [u:]	flown [əu]	fliegen
forbid [i]	forbade [ei]	forbidden [i]	verbieten
forecast [ɑ:]	forecast* [ɑ:]	forecast* [ɑ:]	voraussagen
forget [e]	forgot [ɔ]	forgotten [ɔ]	vergessen
forsake [ei]	forsook [u]	forsaken [ei]	aufgeben; verlassen
freeze [i:]	froze [əu]	frozen [əu]	(ge)frieren
get [e]	got [ɔ]	got [ɔ] Am. gotten [ɔ]	bekommen
gild [i]	gilt* [i]	gilt* [i]	vergolden
gird [ə:]	girt* [ə:]	girt* [ə:]	(um)gürten
give [i]	gave [ei]	given [i]	geben
go [əu]	went [e]	gone [ɔ]	gehen
grind [ai]	ground [au]	ground [au]	mahlen
grow [əu]	grew [u:]	grown [əu]	wachsen; anbauen
hang [æ]	hung* [ʌ]	hung* [ʌ]	(auf)hängen
have [æ, ə]	had [æ, ə]	had [æ, ə]	haben
hear [iə]	heard [ə:]	heard [ə:]	hören
hew [u:]	hewed [u:]	hewn* [u:]	hauen, hacken
hide [ai]	hid [i]	hid(den) [i]	(sich) verstecken
hit [i]	hit [i]	hit [i]	treffen; schlagen
hold [əu]	held [e]	held [e]	halten
hurt [ə:]	hurt [ə:]	hurt [ə:]	verletzen
keep [i:]	kept [e]	kept [e]	(be)halten; aufbewahren
kneel [i:]	knelt* [e]	knelt* [e]	knien
knit [i]	knit* [i]	knit* [i]	stricken
know [əu]	knew [u:]	known [əu]	wissen, kennen

infinitive	past	past participle	
lay [ei]	laid [ei]	laid [ei]	legen
lead [iː]	led [e]	led [e]	führen, leiten
lean [iː]	leant* [e]	leant* [e]	(sich) (an)lehnen
leap [iː]	leapt* [e]	leapt* [e]	(über)springen
learn [əː]	learnt* [əː]	learnt* [əː]	lernen; erfahren
leave [iː]	left [e]	left [e]	(ver)lassen
lend [e]	lent [e]	lent [e]	leihen
let [e]	let [e]	let [e]	lassen
lie [ai]	lay [ei]	lain [ei]	liegen
light [ai]	lit* [i]	lit* [i]	anzünden, erleuchten
lose [uː]	lost [ɔ]	lost [ɔ]	verlieren
make [ei]	made [ei]	made [ei]	machen
mean [iː]	meant [e]	meant [e]	meinen; bedeuten
meet [iː]	met [e]	met [e]	begegnen, treffen
mow [əu]	mowed [əu]	mown* [əu]	mähen
pay [ei]	paid [ei]	paid [ei]	(be)zahlen
put [u]	put [u]	put [u]	legen, stellen, setzen
read [iː]	read [e]	read [e]	lesen
rend [e]	rent [e]	rent [e]	(zer)reißen
rid [i]	rid* [i]	rid [i]	freimachen, befreien
ride [ai]	rode [əu]	ridden [i]	reiten
ring [i]	rang [æ]	rung [ʌ]	läuten
rise [ai]	rose [əu]	risen [i]	aufstehen; aufgehen (von Gestirnen)
rive [ai]	rived [ai]	riven* [i]	(sich) spalten
run [ʌ]	ran [æ]	run [ʌ]	laufen, rennen
saw [ɔː]	sawed [ɔː]	sawn* [ɔː]	sägen
say [ei]	said [e]	said [e]	sagen
see [iː]	saw [ɔː]	seen [iː]	sehen
seek [iː]	sought [ɔː]	sought [ɔː]	suchen
sell [e]	sold [əu]	sold [əu]	verkaufen
send [e]	sent [e]	sent [e]	senden, schicken
set [e]	set [e]	set [e]	setzen, stellen
sew [əu]	sewed [əu]	sewn* [əu]	nähen
shake [ei]	shook [u]	shaken [ei]	schütteln
shear [iə]	sheared [iə]	shorn* [ɔː]	scheren
shed [e]	shed [e]	shed [e]	vergießen
shine [ai]	shone [ɔ]	shone [ɔ]	scheinen, glänzen
shoe [uː]	shod [ɔ]	shod [ɔ]	(Pferd) beschlagen
shoot [uː]	shot [ɔ]	shot [ɔ]	schießen

infinitive	past	past participle	
show [əu]	showed [əu]	shown [əu]	zeigen
shred [e]	shred* [e]	shred* [e]	(zer)schnitzeln, zerfetzen
shrink [i]	shrank [æ]	shrunk [ʌ]	einschrumpfen
shut [ʌ]	shut [ʌ]	shut [ʌ]	schließen
sing [i]	sang [æ]	sung [ʌ]	singen
sink [i]	sank [æ]	sunk [ʌ]	sinken
sit [i]	sat [æ]	sat [æ]	sitzen
slay [ei]	slew [u:]	slain [ei]	erschlagen
sleep [i:]	slept [e]	slept [e]	schlafen
slide [ai]	slid [i]	slid [i]	gleiten
sling [i]	slung [ʌ]	slung [ʌ]	schleudern
slink [i]	slunk [ʌ]	slunk [ʌ]	schleichen
slit [i]	slit [i]	slit [i]	schlitzen
smell [e]	smelt* [e]	smelt* [e]	riechen
smite [ai]	smote [əu]	smitten [i],	schlagen
sow [əu]	sowed [əu]	sown* [əu]	(aus)säen
speak [i:]	spoke [əu]	spoken [əu]	sprechen
speed [i:]	sped* [e]	sped* [e]	eilen
spell [e]	spelt* [e]	spelt* [e]	buchstabieren
spend [e]	spent [e]	spent [e]	ausgeben
spill [i]	spilt* [i]	spilt* [i]	verschütten
spin [i]	spun [ʌ], span [æ]	spun [ʌ]	spinnen
spit [i]	spat [æ]	spat [æ]	spucken
split [i]	split [i]	split [i]	spalten
spoil [ɔi]	spoilt* [ɔi]	spoilt* [ɔi]	verderben
spread [e]	spread [e]	spread [e]	verbreiten
spring [i]	sprang [æ]	sprung [ʌ]	springen
stand [æ]	stood [u]	stood [u]	stehen
steal [i:]	stole [əu]	stolen [əu]	stehlen
stick [i]	stuck [ʌ]	stuck [ʌ]	stecken
sting [i]	stung [ʌ]	stung [ʌ]	stechen
stink [i]	stank [æ]	stunk [ʌ]	stinken
strew [u:]	strewed [u:]	strewn* [u:]	(be)streuen
stride [ai]	strode [əu]	stridden [i]	über-, durch- schreiten
strike [ai]	struck [ʌ]	struck [ʌ]	schlagen
string [i]	strung [ʌ]	strung [ʌ]	spannen
strive [ai]	strove [əu]	striven [i]	streben
swear [ɛə]	swore [ɔ:]	sworn [ɔ:]	schwören
sweep [i:]	swept [e]	swept [e]	fegen
swell [e]	swelled [e]	swollen* [əu]	(an)schwellen
swim [i]	swam [æ]	swum [ʌ]	schwimmen
swing [i]	swung [ʌ]	swung [ʌ]	schwingen
take [ei]	took [u]	taken [ei]	nehmen
teach [i:]	taught [ɔ:]	taught [ɔ:]	lehren

infinitive	past	past participle	
tear [ɛə]	tore [ɔː]	torn [ɔː]	ziehen
tell [e]	told [əu]	told [əu]	sagen
think [i]	thought [ɔː]	thought [ɔː]	denken
thrive [ai]	throve* [əu]	thriven* [i]	gedeihen
throw [əu]	threw [uː]	thrown [əu]	werfen
thrust [ʌ]	thrust [ʌ]	thrust [ʌ]	stoßen
tread [e]	trod [ɔ]	trod(den) [ɔ]	treten
wake [ei]	woke* [əu]	woke* [əu]	wachen
wear [ɛə]	wore [ɔː]	worn [ɔː]	(Kleider) tragen
weave [iː]	wove [əu]	woven [əu]	weben
weep [iː]	wept [e]	wept [e]	weinen
wet [e]	wet* [e]	wet* [e]	nässen
win [i]	won [ʌ]	won [ʌ]	gewinnen
wind [ai]	wound [au]	wound [au]	winden
wring [i]	wrung [ʌ]	wrung [ʌ]	(aus)wringen
write [ai]	wrote [əu]	written [i]	schreiben

2. Alphabetische Liste
der einzelnen Stammformen

abide
abode s. abide
arise
arisen s. arise
arose s. arise
ate s. eat
awake
awaken s. awake
awoke s. awake

bade s. bid
be
bear
beat
beaten s. beat
became s. become
become
been s. be
began s. begin
beget
begin
begot s. beget
begotten s. beget
begun s. begin
bend
bent s. bend
beseech
besought
  s. beseech
bet
bid
bide
bind
bit s. bite
bite
bitten s. bite
bled s. bleed
bleed
blew s. blow
blow
blown s. blow
bode s. bide
bore s. bear
born s. bear
borne s. bear
bought s. buy

bound s. bind
break
bred s. breed
breed
bring
broke s. break
broken s. break
brought s. bring
build
built s. build
burn
burnt s. burn
burst
buy

came s. come
cast
catch
caught s. catch
chid s. chide
chidden s. chide
chide
choose
chose s. choose
chosen s. choose
cleave
cleft s. cleave
cling
clove s. cleave
cloven s. cleave
clung s. cling
come
cost
creep
crept s. creep
cut

deal
dealt s. deal
did s. do
dig
do
done s. do
drank s. drink
draw
drawn s. draw

dream
dreamt s. dream
drew s. draw
drink
drive
driven s. drive
drove s. drive
drunk s. drink
dug s. dig
dwell
dwelt s. dwell

eat
eaten s. eat

fall
fallen s. fall
fed s. feed
feed
feel
fell s. fall
felt s. feel
fight
find
fled s. flee
flee
flew s. fly
fling
flown s. fly
flung s. fling
fly
forbade s. forbid
forbid
forbidden
  s. forbid
forecast
forget
forgot s. forget
forgotten
  s. forget
forsake
forsaken
  s. forsake
forsook s. forsake
fought s. fight
found s. find

freeze
froze s. freeze
frozen s. freeze

gave s. give
get
gild
gilt s. gild
gird
girt s. gird
give
given s. give
go
gone s. go
got s. get
gotten s. get
grew s. grow
grind
ground s. grind
grow
grown s. grow

had s. have
hang
have
hear
heard s. hear
held s. hold
hew
hewn s. hew
hid s. hide
hidden s. hide
hide
hit
hold
hung s. hang
hurt

keep
kept s. keep
kneel
knelt s. kneel
knew s. know
knit
know
known s. know

laid s. lay
lain s. lie
lay

lay s. lie
lead
lean
leant s. lean
leap
leapt s. leap
learn
learnt s. learn
leave
led s. lead
left s. leave
lend
lent s. lend
let
lie
light
lit s. light
lose
lost s. lose

made s. make
make
mean
meant s. mean
meet
met s. meet
mow
mown s. mow

paid s. pay
pay
put

ran s. run
rang s. ring
read
rend
rent s. rend
rid
ridden s. ride
ride
ring
rise
risen s. rise
rive
riven s. rive
rode s. ride
rose s. rise
run
rung s. ring

said s. say
sang s. sing
sank s. sink
sat s. sit
saw
saw s. see
sawn s. saw
say
see
seek
seen s. see
sell
send
sent s. send
set
sew
sewn s. sew
shake
shaken s. shake
shear
shed
shine
shod s. shoe
shoe
shone s. shine
shook s. shake
shoot
shorn
shot s. shoot
show
shown s. show
shrank s. shrink
shred
shrink
shrunk s. shrink
shut
sing
sink
sit
slain s. slay
slay
sleep
slept s. sleep
slew s. slay
slid s. slide
slide
sling
slink
slit
slung s. sling

slunk s. slink
smell
smelt s. smell
smite
smitten s. smite
sold s. sell
sought s. seek
sow
sown s. sow
span s. spin
spat s. spit
speak
sped s. speed
speed
spell
spelt s. spell
spend
spent s. spend
spill
spilt s. spill
spin
spit
split
spoil
spoilt s. spoil
spoke s. speak
spoken s. speak
sprang s. spring
spread
spring
sprung s. spring
spun s. spin
stand
stank s. stink
steal
stick
sting
stink
stole s. steal
stolen s. steal

stood s. stand
strew
strewn s. strew
stridden
  s. stride
stride
strike
string
strive
striven s. strive
strode s. stride
strove s. strive
struck s. strike
strung s. string
stuck s. stick
stung s. sting
stunk s. stink
sung s. sing
sunk s. sink
swam s. swim
swear
sweep
swell
swept s. sweep
swim
swing
swollen s. swell
swore s. swear
sworn s. swear
swum s. swim
swung s. swing

take
taken s. take
taught s. teach
teach
tear
tell
think
thought s. think

threw s. throw
thrive
thriven s. thrive
throve s. thrive
throw
thrown s. throw
thrust
told s. tell
took s. take
tore s. tear
torn s. tear
tread
trod s. tread
trodden s. tread

wake
was s. be
wear
weave
weep
went s. go
wept s. weep
were s. be
wet
win
wind
woke s. wake
woken s. wake
won s. win
wore s. wear
worn s. wear
wound s. wind
wove s. weave
woven
  s. weave
wring
write
written s. write
wrote s. write
wrung s. wring